Campus Critic

The Architecture of the University of Nottingham

A Peter Fawcett
and
Neil Jackson

Campus Critique

The Architecture of the
University of Nottingham

Typeset in Frutiger and Printed by
The Sherwood Press (Nottingham) Limited
Hadden Court, Glaisdale Parkway, Glaisdale Drive West, Nottingham, England.

Published by The Sherwood Press (Nottingham) Limited.

ISBN 0 948983 05 1

CONTENTS

ACKNOWLEDGEMENTS

Every book, such as this, is a collaborative effort. Without the help of many people both within and without the University community, such a venture would not have come to fruition. The authors, therefore, are particularly indebted to the Vice-Chancellor, Professor Sir Colin Campbell, for promoting this study and for writing the Foreword; to the former Registrar, David Allen, for providing the support which made the book possible and the brief for an "accessible" text, which we hope we have met; to Chris Jagger, Director of Estate Management and to the University's Estate Office, for allowing us free access to their records and archives; and, similarly, to Dr Dorothy Johnston, Keeper of the University Library's Department of Manuscripts and Special Collections. Across the campuses at Highfields and Sutton Bonington, and in both the Queen's Medical Centre and the City Hospital, Hall Wardens, Heads of Schools and those many people responsible for a wide range of facilities have allowed us to invade, note and photograph their territory. To all we are extremely grateful.

Writing this book has taught us a lot about the place where we work, and this learning experience has been made particularly enjoyable due to the great kindness and keen interest of the first Vice-Chancellor, Bertrand Hallward. We only hope that we have drawn a fair and balanced picture of his vision.

We would also like to thank, for their various observations and contributions: Ken Brand; Professor Dan Eley; Hugh Ellwood of Building Design Partnership; Bob Gibbs, Director of the University of Nottingham Regional Unit; Sir Michael Hopkins; Matthew Letts; Fiona Newton; Dr Taner Oc; M G O'Donoghue, Head of Estates at The Nottingham Trent University; Dr Ernie Scoffham; Edward Stronell; and Professor Brian Tate.

Finally, we would also like to express our indebtedness to those who helped in the actual preparation of the book: to the British Architectural Library, RIBA, London, for permission to reproduce illustrations from their collection; to our photographers, Martine Hamilton-Knight, who provided all the colour plates used in the book, as well as a number of black and white photographs, and to Glyn Halls, for his black and white photography; to James Baker, who prepared two drawings of the new campus for the Postscript; to Alyster Jackson who read and corrected the final manuscript; to Sue Davies who prepared the index; and to Gordon Hudson and Steve Summers of our publishers, The Sherwood Press, whose design and production expertise has steered this book to fruition. Without their considerable contribution, this book would have been a far thinner and less appealing volume.

FOREWORD

Since the granting of the University of Nottingham's Royal Charter in 1948, the Highfields campus has seen five decades of remarkable achievement. We have moved from the status of a small University College to become one of the most successful and respected universities in the United Kingdom, with a reputation reaching well beyond our shores. We enjoy great popularity with well-qualified and well-motivated students, and have established a research base which boasts more top-rated departments than any institution outside Oxbridge and London. This success is reflected in the landscape, architecture and number of landmark buildings on our campus. There is no doubt, as can be seen by the use made of these buildings today, that they have stood the test of time and have been adaptable and flexible in meeting the changing needs of their users.

My belief is that the University's success is due in no small measure to the fact that throughout its history, it has had the vision to look forward and, while respecting tradition, has also accepted the need for change. The University has had the courage to invest while others were retrenching, and to focus its efforts on the areas in which it could demonstrate an ability to deliver research and teaching of an international standard. Higher Education continues to face many difficult challenges, notably the need for new means of funding the expansion of student numbers that is generally agreed to be essential to ensure the future competitiveness of the nation. The University of Nottingham has already, by its investment in a new campus, committed itself to lead a resurgence of confidence in higher education. The new campus, designed by Michael Hopkins and Partners, is due to welcome its first students in October 1999. Located on a former industrial estate within a mile of the University, it will feature a prominent lake and lakeside promenade reminiscent of Highfields.

As the University expands, we remain dedicated to preserving and enhancing the beauty of our existing Highfields campus, not only for students and staff, but also for the enjoyment of all the people of Nottingham.

Professor Sir Colin Campbell
Vice-Chancellor

Introduction

Fifty years on from receiving its Royal Charter in 1948, the University of Nottingham is now considered as one of Britain's 'older' universities. Whilst this may be attributed to the 1992 Higher Education Act and the plethora of 'new' universities established in its wake, such new-found status after a mere half-century also indicates that historically, university expansion in Britain is but a recent phenomenon.

Until the nineteenth century Oxford and Cambridge were the only universities in England. Even by the outbreak of the Second World War, the University Grants Committee, founded in 1919, could only muster Oxford and Cambridge, a handful of northern civics and the Celtic universities. The later civic universities, of which Nottingham was the first to receive its charter, were postwar foundations from 1948 (Nottingham) to 1955 (Exeter); all had grown from their previous university college status offering external London degrees. Until the 1992 Act, however, it was the 1960s which witnessed the most rapid university expansion in our history; during the decade student numbers rose from 100,000 to 220,000 with an attendant increase in universities from 22 to 46. Such was the response to Lord Robbins' report published in October 1963 to "review the pattern of full-time education", resulting not only in a series of new 'campus' universities generally sited well outside their associated towns or cities, but also in considerable expansion of existing foundations such as Nottingham.

The origins of Nottingham University, as of, for example, the universities of Bristol, Sheffield, and Reading, lie in the Cambridge 'extension lectures', an enlightened scheme devised in 1866 by a Cambridge don, James Stuart, to bring the benefits of Cambridge teaching to a wider provincial audience. Such was the response in Nottingham that in 1875 the Town Council received a gift of £10,000 from a local wealthy, but anonymous, lace manufacturer to establish a University College. The Council referred the donation to a special committee which resolved to build a new college to meet the requirements of the benefactor, and the perceived educational needs of the town, on a town centre site at Horse Fair Close, with easy access for most of the town's population. Opened in early July 1881 by Prince Leopold, Duke of Albany, amidst considerable pomp and ceremony, for instruction in "those branches of knowledge which are capable of practical application in the various industrial pursuits [of the region]", the new University College represented a fitting climax to the determination of the local Mechanics' Institute, formalised at a meeting a decade previously, "... to establish classes at which working men might have facilities for obtaining instruction in those subjects most important for them as artisans, fathers of families, and sharers in the political power of the country." (*The Builder*, 25 June 1881).

Such university colleges were to find appropriate expression in their architecture. Manchester and Liverpool had the wit to commission that doyen of northern Victorian gothic revivalists, Alfred Waterhouse, architect of Manchester Town Hall and, later, London's Natural History Museum; Birmingham engaged the eclectic Aston Webb, architect to the Victoria and Albert Museum and Admiralty Arch, albeit much against the wishes of the first principal, Sir Oliver Lodge, who argued that buildings alone did not make a university. But the response from that college's chief protagonist, Joseph Chamberlain, was swift and prescient: "No, spend the money now, give people something to see". Nottingham's University College in Shakespeare Street, begun in 1877 by another firm of committed northern gothicists, W and R Mawson, had similar aspirations to civic monumentality and indeed, predictably, was met with less than critical acclaim in some quarters; its most celebrated alumnus, D H Lawrence, depicted University College in *The Rainbow,* dismissing its gothic revivalism as "foolish". Indeed, it could be argued that Mawson's particular brand of civic gothic had become somewhat outmoded by the time of its completion in 1881. But within half a century, University College was to be relocated well outside the town centre in a new parkland setting at Highfields; moreover, a dramatic shift to classicism as the accepted expression applied to inter-war buildings for higher education, inevitably produced a profoundly modified paradigm, where the juxtaposition of classical architecture and mature, informal landscape combined to reflect a new twentieth-century orthodoxy for university building.

By 1920, Jesse Boot, the pharmacist, had acquired the Highfields estate in south-west Nottingham to the west of Lenton village. His original intention had been to establish on this site an autonomous industrial community on the lines of Bourneville or Port Sunlight, but by the following year he revealed a philanthropic plan wherein the site was to be given over to a public park with lake, and for the building of a new 'palace of education' on a 60 acre campus. A plan to establish a new University of the Midlands on this site was thwarted but a new University College, still the visual focus and administrative centre of the current university, was officially opened by George V in 1928.

The provenance for such a university model, classical pavilions judiciously placed within an arcadian landscape, had been established in the early nineteenth century; William Wilkins' new quadrangle at Downing College, Cambridge, in 1807, had incorporated the discoveries of progressive eighteenth century landscape design, and the Downing model had been adopted with spectacular success by Thomas Jefferson for a whole university at Charlottesville, Virginia, from 1817. Moreover, further evidence of Nottingham's 'campus' idea had emerged contemporaneously with the move of Exeter's college to parkland at Streatham estate in 1922, and with the establishment of university colleges at Leicester and Hull as campuses in 1921 and 1926 respectively.

For the new University College at Highfields Jesse Boot not surprisingly engaged his favourite architect, Morley Horder. Horder was a typical English architectural practitioner of the day; untainted by any new-fangled notions of Continental modernism, Horder's predilections were essentially traditional and eclectic. He was at ease variously with half-timbered shop interiors for Boots Cash Chemists, country houses or suburban villas in the 'Cotswold' style, or, indeed, with his (later) historicist additions to Oxbridge colleges. When faced with the design of a major civic monument like University College, he turned, as most of his contemporaries would have done, to tradition and more specifically to the classical language of architecture. For all its fundamental flaws in the area of functional planning, University College (or Trent Building as it became known in acknowledgement of Jesse Boot's subsequent ennoblement) still maintains its primacy as the most potent physical symbol of a regional university, in spite of seventy years' building activity at Highfields since its completion. Horder went on to design not only Florence Boot Hall of residence for women, a largely mundane confection in stripped neo-Georgian, but also an open-air lido and an 'Italianate' Lakeside Pavilion for the public park.

But within a decade there was the Munich crisis and the threat of war. The Second World War halted the steady development of higher education in Britain; denuded of students during the war years, universities were left in 1945 with a huge demand for places not only to fill a backlog of deferred entry but also to meet the demands of the Ministry of Labour and National Service that ninety percent of places should be filled by ex-servicemen. Such measures were to increase the full-time student population in British universities from 50,000 in 1938 to 82,000 in 1954.

It was within this climate of postwar optimism that Bertrand Hallward was appointed as Principal of University College in 1947. By August, 1948, University College, Nottingham, had received its Charter and had achieved full university status with Hallward installed as the first Vice-Chancellor. Bertrand Hallward was to emerge as the greatest single influence upon the physical development of Highfields. Not surprisingly, in view of his provenance (Haileybury and Peterhouse, built respectively by the classicists Wilkins and Burrough, and Clifton College in the Puginian gothic of Hansom), his architectural predilections were overtly traditional. Moreover, Hallward inherited at Nottingham an established 'campus' tradition of classical monuments within the landscape; the subsequent development, then, of brick neo-Georgian halls of residence carefully placed within the Highfields 'down' seemed a logical and

natural outcome of what had gone before. It was also an outcome carefully orchestrated by Sir Percy Thomas, whom Hallward had appointed in 1948 to prepare a campus development plan when university status was granted. Thomas by this time was a senior figure of the British architectural establishment having completed two years previously his second term as President of the Royal Institute of British Architects. He remained an entrenched traditionalist at a time when younger members of his profession were looking to progressive developments in Europe, the United States, and Scandinavia for their architectural inspiration. Thomas' plan was considerably modified by Britain's most prominent and prolific twentieth-century landscape architect, G A Jellicoe, in 1955. Jellicoe remained sensitive to the provenance of Nottingham's 'campus' idea and reached a convincing compromise between tradition and modernity. Even by 1963 it was still deemed to be "an exemplary plan" by the influential *Architectural Review*.

But the same journal had previously equivocated over some of the more traditionalist elements retained in Jellicoe's plan; in October 1957 the *Architectural Review* devoted an issue to recent university buildings unflatteringly referring to Nottingham's efforts as "Banker's Georgian". Nor did the 'campus' model gain support from the progressive architectural press; Nottingham's campus, along with Aberdeen, Reading and Keele were categorised as "isolationist" in the same issue where low density development was likened, in equal terms of derogation, to the contemporaneous New Towns. Even by 1963, when the post-Robbins 'new' universities had adopted the campus orthodoxy, the same journal had not tempered its hostility. Still peddling the "isolationist" charge, Lionel Brett, declared, "Any activity which takes itself outside of [sic] the city . . . impoverishes the city and impoverishes itself. For the city it is the loss of youth in its streets . . . of variety and vitality in the townscape. For the university it is the subtle threat of a new kind of public school segregation."

But the modernists ultimately had their say. Even traditionalists like Hallward conceded, along with Jellicoe, that proposals for a new complex of science and engineering buildings on level ground at the east of the campus might best be served by architects from the progressive camp. The result was a range of distinguished buildings all firmly within the 'modernist' idiom to a development plan prepared in 1957 by Basil Spence. A Scot, Spence had gained national acclaim from his competition-winning entry for Coventry Cathedral in 1950 (completed in 1962) and for his major exhibition pavilions at the 1951 Festival of Britain. His plan at Nottingham for 'Science City' as it became affectionately known, was completed by his associate, Andrew Renton. Spence introduced to Highfields a quintessentially English expression of mainstream modern architecture acceptable to progressives and traditionalists alike. His contribution offered a welcome relief from the established pursuit of a faded classical tradition which lived on in a central area development plan submitted to the university by Donald McMorran in 1958. In the event, this scheme promoted a series of loosely defined hierarchical quadrangles enclosed by typically well-mannered buildings carefully detailed in traditional materials, just as the same architect had proposed for Cripps Hall of residence, but a far cry from Spence's simultaneous modernist pursuits at the Clifton Boulevard site.

One significant aspect of the McMorran scheme was the judicious siting of a monumental assembly hall-*cum*-theatre between the Trent Building and what was to become the Portland Building. This hugely-scaled and colonnaded building would have established a satisfactory visual link between its two firmly classical but isolated neighbours by the simple expedient of presenting a massive unadorned gable to the 'gap' between Trent and Portland. The problem of this unresolved 'no man's land' was to exercise architects' imaginations for decades to come; the 1989 insertion of the bungaloid Institute of German, Austrian and Swiss Affairs (now the Graduate School) by architects Bartlett, Gray and Partners, was, on account of its diminutive scale, a miserably unfitting response.

The 1960s also saw the gestation of the next major university development at Nottingham, the establishment of a Medical School and Teaching Hospital, completed in 1979. The huge complex, designed by Building Design Partnership according to progressive transatlantic practice, was a further acknowledgement that so-called modernism had come to stay, and that such a demanding brief could not be satisfied by an outmoded traditional architecture. By contrast, Sheffield's Hallamshire Hospital by Adams, Holden and Pearson, was a traditional Beaux Arts design won in competition in 1939, but not completed until 1971.

British universities underwent a period of consolidation in the 1970s and 1980s and Nottingham was no exception; apart from the Medical School and Hallward Library for arts and social sciences designed by Faulkner-Brown, Hendy, Watkinson and Stonor, the period is characterised not by ambitious development proposals but by modest interventions to existing building stock and by new buildings stitched into a well-established campus model. Some were sensitive to this ethos and its architectural precepts, particularly the prosecution of Spence's plan by his successor, Andrew Renton. Others, notably Cartwright, Woollatt and Partners' extensions to Cripps and Derby Halls of residence emerged as banal pastiches of distinguished precedents; similarly misguided was F S Eales and Partners' extension to Florence Boot Hall in 1971 which merely reiterated Morley Horder's bland neo-Georgian design of 1929.

The next fifteen years at Highfields were characterised by further insertion of new buildings and by considerable re-ordering of existing buildings to meet not only the rapidly changing requirements of a modern university, particularly, for example, in computing and laboratory provision, but also the upgrading of outworn and obsolete building stock. Significant developments included the Highfields Science Park, Broadgate student housing, an Institute of Hearing Research, a new Magnetic Resonance building and most particularly the Djanogly Arts Centre, by the Graham Brown Partnership, completed in 1992. The Arts Centre, along with the adjacent Department of Music and Recital Hall by the same architect, replaced Morley Horder's open-air lido designed firmly within the Tuscan idiom. Taking on fashionable post-modern concerns, the architects not only invoked the 'memory' of a demolished forbear by using similarly antique rotunda and basilica forms, but 'dressed' the building in debased classical detail. This merely demonstrates how, after half a century, the building stock of an institution such as the University of Nottingham inevitably expresses not only the aspirations of those responsible for its building procurement, but, in microcosm, reflects the development of mainstream late-twentieth-century British architecture.

As we approach the Millennium, there are signs that the campus vision, initiated by Bertrand Hallward in 1948, is to be maintained and amplified; an architectural competition instigated in 1996 by Vice-Chancellor Sir Colin Campbell for a new university campus on a disused gearbox factory site adjacent to Highfields has produced a strategic plan of great ambition. Winning architect Sir Michael Hopkins has designed a collection of discrete buildings which not only promise a sustainable architecture well beyond the University's centenary, but also, by reinterpreting that English tradition of buildings within the landscape, offer a telling reiteration of Bertrand Hallward's vision of fifty years previously.

Chapter 1
The Origins of the University

Shakespeare Street

The architectural development of the University of Nottingham began, as it did with many grand civic universities, with a single, purpose-built college building in the city centre. Founded in 1877 and completed in 1881, this building was eventually deserted for the Highfields estate in 1928, and it now serves as the Arkwright Building of the Nottingham Trent University.

The University College in Shakespeare Street was a building which spoke clearly of its civic purpose. Its appearance today is not the result of negligence, but of a direct bomb hit by the Luftwaffe in May 1941. The building has been rebuilt, but with modesty, and if the interiors appear blandly institutional, the gables naked of sculpture and the windows devoid of stained glass, it is perhaps a recognition of the significance of the architectural composition that the building was rebuilt as completely as it was. Another generation might just as soon have demolished it.

The architects for Nottingham's new University College building were the northern firm of W and R Mawson who, as Lockwood and Mawson, had secured a reputation for sensible civic architecture and solid, pragmatic design. Based in Bradford, Henry Francis Lockwood and the brothers William and Richard Mawson, were not part of the high-church, high-art clique which dominated mid-Victorian, London-based architecture, but rather level-headed practitioners in the manner of Manchester's Alfred Waterhouse. Lockwood had moved to London in 1874, while retaining a link with the partnership, but died in 1878. Thus the Arkwright Building was designed, if one consults Pevsner, by

Lockwood and Mawson, yet completed by W and R Mawson. Although the firm's background was in classical buildings, such as St George's Hall, Bradford (1851-52), they had kept up with changes in fashion and had been strongly influenced by the architecture, and presumably the writing - *vide* the Midland Grand Hotel at St Pancras (1868-74) and *Remarks on Secular and Domestic Architecture* (1858) - of George Gilbert Scott, as demonstrated by their Bradford Exchange of 1864-67 and their competition design for the Law Courts of 1866-67. They were the architects of Bradford Town Hall (1869-73), a gothic building reminiscent of the cloth halls of Flanders, a reference not lost upon the mercantile city; and they were also the architects of Saltaire (1851-76), Sir Titus Salt's grid-plan model town, where the school and town hall addressed each other across the main axis, and the factory and congregational church stood symmetrically at either end of the cross axis. Here the workers' houses were neat, terraced and Italianate, and there was not a pub to be found. With such high-minded and well-ordered architects, the governors of the new University College were in good hands.

The town council's choice of architect was significant, for some commentators, like *The Builder,* saw the new University College as "a pile which will in future go far to redeem the unusual poverty of the town as regards municipal architecture." The site, located a stone's throw to the north of Market Street and the porticoed Theatre Royal, was the Horse Fair Close, "a portion of land [as *The Builder* noted] surrounded by new and handsome streets, and yet sufficiently central to meet all the requirements of the population." This was land which had been developed as a result of the Enclosure Act of 1845: the Horse Fair Close had been bought by the Corporation under the Act, and Shakespeare Street built across it in 1852. The site was flanked to the east, across South Sherwood Street, by the cattle market, in which position it was generally thought that the new town hall would be built. This would have placed the University College right in the civic heart of Nottingham. In the event, the cattle market site was given to other civic needs, the magistrates court and the police and fire stations, and the Council House was built by T C Howitt down in Market Square.

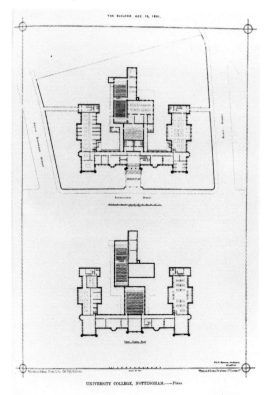

UNIVERSITY COLLEGE, NOTTINGHAM.——Plans.

Like the Queen's College building in Belfast, designed by Charles Lanyon thirty years earlier in 1847, Lockwood and Mawson's design for the new University College adopted an E-shaped plan **[1]**, the long side facing onto

Shakespeare Street to the north, its centrally-placed entrance almost on axis, but not quite, with the Wesleyan Reform Chapel opposite, built by J Simpson of Leeds in 1855 or 1856. But unlike Lanyon's earlier building, with its thin and unconvincing English Perpendicular, Mawson's college assumed a more eclectic style which fell slightly uncomfortably between the muscular forms of thirteenth-century French gothic and the open, repetitive rhythms of the Italian gothic. It was a victim of both but a hostage to neither.

The long, main frontage, the back of the E, was a scaled-down version of what they had done previously at the Bradford Town Hall, yet similar in almost all aspects of arrangement, composition and detail. It was an elevation dominated by three cross gables 60ft (18.2m) high, the central one, flanked by squat, polygonal towers, presenting a triple-hooded doorway and three linked windows above, decorated with geometrical tracery, to Shakespeare Street. Over the window, the tympanum, decorated with diaper work, supported three broad bands of sculpture representing a school of students of the arts and sciences, and three medallions in high relief showing Sculpture, Painting and Music. Surmounted by a leaded flèche rising to 120ft (36.5m), this was an imposing entrance and some counterpoint to the heavy horizontality of the 260ft (80m) long façade. Its details were French, reminiscent of the cathedrals of northern France, but the broad horizontality of its composition, enforced by the linked lancets which ran, as an arcade, almost the full length of the upper storey, was north Italian and not without educational precedent, recalling both the Doge's Palace in Venice and James

Wild's more recent St Martin's in the Fields Northern District School in Holborn, London of 1849-50. Against each of the three gables and standing upon squat pedestals, were statues of six worthies, each 7ft 6ins (2.3m) tall, carved by Farmer and Brindley of Westminster: Shakespeare and Milton to the left, Bacon and Newton at the centre, and Watt and Cuvier to the right. But the bombing of 1941 has done away with the last two.

Science, as four of these worthies do suggest, was the main purpose of this building. Behind the right-hand gable, and facing onto Bilbie Street, were the vertebrate and invertebrate museums arranged respectively on two floors: hence Georges Cuvier. Behind the central gable and beyond the galleried entrance hall with its flanking classrooms, and in a larger mass of building than the frontage would suggest, were theatres for chemical, physical and general lectures together with professors' rooms and laboratories. Here James Watt, Isaac Newton and Francis Bacon were accommodated. The third gable, given to John Milton and William Shakespeare, symbolised literature, for the South Sherwood Street wing contained the Free Public Library with a newsroom and central reading room on the ground floor, and a reading room and reference library on the floor above. Thus the building contained three distinct functions, each façade a composed elevation and each part separate and, in terms of access and circulation, apart from the rest.

But behind the stained glass and Ancaster stone of the street façades, the rear of the building, constructed of yellow brick with red brick trim, was considerably more reserved. A tall, campanile-like chimney, an early addition, recalls the Italianate gothic of the frontage but the message is always utilitarian. The E-plan afforded good ventilation to the various public rooms, lecture theatres and laboratories which overlooked the rear courts, a convenience which was not missed in the positioning and isolating of the toilets as single-storey blocks where each cubicle had its own window and each urinal, patented by George Jennings of Palace Wharf, Lambeth, offered gentlemen a target ring.

Spaciousness and ventilation were also apparent inside, where the ceilings were high, due to the use of gas lamps, and where, in the reference library and invertebrate museum, rooms which measured 90ft long by 45ft wide (27 by 13.5m), the roof structure was left exposed to reveal a complex arrangement of thin wrought iron rods, cast iron shafts and connecting rings forming braced trusses of daring fragility. "All these apartments", as *The Builder* observed, "are fitted with the newest improvements, and no effort has been spared to render them complete." Lifts (presumably dumb-waiters rather than passenger lifts) connected the basement service rooms with the upper floors of the two flanking wings while in the centre wing, the largest lecture theatre, which was intended for "popular lectures upon scientific subjects" and could seat 600 people, was "illuminated from the roof by two sunlights, which are lighted by means of an electric battery". Here too were located the Chemical Theatre, which could accommodate 220 students, and the Physical Theatre, with seats for 100. Attached to the latter was the balance room where solid rock, part of the foundation of the building, provided a firm and vibration-free base for the balance table. Elsewhere, the 125ft (38m) long optical gallery, "said [according to *The Builder*] to be one of the finest in the kingdom", provided for experiments with light.

Despite the high standard of these facilities, the architectural richness suggested by the façade progressed no further than the entrance hall, with its canopied and crested fireplace, and the surrounding gallery, with some strap-work on the ceiling and stiff-leaf in the capitals. Yet it was an interior which appealed to Ursula, D H Lawrence's heroine of *The Rainbow:* "She liked the hall, with its big stone chimney-piece and its Gothic arches supporting the balcony above", even though "the arches were ugly, [and] the chimney-piece of cardboard-like carved stone, with its armorial decoration, looked silly just opposite the bicycle stand and the radiator." Whatever its appearance, the new University College, built at a cost of £70,000, was found to be unstable and in 1883, after two years' use, it was closed again. In March 1884, the Town Council met and the defects of the new building were reported upon. It was claimed that the specification had not been carried out and that the architects had delegated responsibility to a foreman carpenter. "Mr Young", *The Architect* reported, "stated that the building was in such deplorable condition that he was told that in ten years' time the building would tumble down unless something very urgent was done." Something *was* done and the building reopened in 1890. Meanwhile, it was agreed that the question of cost should be settled by arbitration.

Fig. 2
Angelo Terrace
14-20 Shakespeare Street
Nottingham
Architect: R Clarke
1853-1854

Adult Education

Although the University College moved out of Shakespeare Street in 1928, handing Lockwood and Mawson's grand civic pile over to the City, there remained still a vestige of Nottingham's first university close to its original site. Across Shakespeare Street the Department of Adult Education, founded in 1920, had occupied a rather curious building, incrementally, since 1925. In 1922 the University College had bought Nos. 14, 16, 18 and 20 Shakespeare Street, four decayed mid-Victorian houses hiding behind a grand and now Listed façade [2]. No. 14 was the first to be occupied but the whole was not taken over until 1950, when the tenants of the remaining house, No. 20, eventually vacated. The remodelled building was opened, by the Archbishop of York, as the University Adult Education Centre, in May 1952. The following history of this building has been researched by Margaret Goodchild, a student of that department.

As has been noted, Shakespeare Street was laid out in 1852, and the first reference to Nos. 14 to 20 Shakespeare Street comes in the *Directory* of 1855, when they appear as Angelo Terrace. This suggests that they were built in 1853 or 1854. The occupants of the four houses were Mr R Clarke, an architect; Mr T Simpson, another architect; Mr T Simpson, again, but now listed as a builder; and Mr R C Bourne, a surgeon. From this it could be surmised that Angelo Terrace was built by Mr Simpson, possibly in partnership with Mr Clarke. But by 1858 Mr Clarke had moved out and Mr D Lynam, of the building firm of Simpson and Lynam, had moved in. Such occupancies are indicative of the processes of speculative building.

Angelo Terrace looks very much like a speculative development. It is an example of what might be called the "palace façade": a grand façade, purporting to be one house but in fact accommodating many. Thus each leaseholder (for such developments were almost always leasehold) could pretend to the ownership of the whole building for but one fourth, in this case, of the real cost. Such conceits helped the building to sell, and that was the business of the speculative builder.

As with house-builders today, speculative builders were usually conservative and rarely at the forefront of current architectural thinking. As an example of their work, Angelo Terrace is no exception. Its pedimented, Palladian elevation suggests the town and even country houses of the 18th century, but its unorthodoxy belies its authenticity. The red bricks are smooth and probably machine-made: the Brick Tax had been lifted only in 1850, immediately encouraging the production and use of this material. The stone quoins and heavy cornice withhold the façade, like a drawing stretched across a drawing board, and give no indication that the achitecture is any more than surface deep. Indeed, the rusticated distyle-in-antis portico appears to be applied to the brick skin behind. The proportions are not altogether comfortable, the three-storey portico appearing rather pinched and the side bays rather empty, although the window architraves and first floor sill band do something to alleviate this. There was, apparently, a large statue of Michaelangelo in the centre of the elevation, although its exact location is now hard to determine. Perhaps this was intended to give the building some dignity: in the event it did at least give it its name, Angelo Terrace.

Chapter 2
**The Buildings on the Highfields
and Lenton Park Estates**

The Highfields Estate

There is little congruity in the collection of older houses and outbuildings which make up the Highfields site. Purchased in a piecemeal fashion, mostly after the University College opened in 1928, they present a varied although architecturally coherent picture of late-eighteenth and late-nineteenth century rural and suburban house building. The best buildings were taken immediately into the confines of the new university campus; the lesser ones, located along the Derby Road on what was the Lenton Park Estate, and on the top of the downs, at the termination of Lenton Hall Drive, were gradually absorbed as their suburban fences and hedges gave way to lawns and tarmac.

The two earliest and most outstanding buildings on the Highfields site, Lenton Hall (now Hugh Stewart Hall) **[3]** and Highfield House **[4]**, are less interesting

Fig. 3

Lenton Hall (now Hugh Stewart Hall)
1792

for what they are than for what they might be. Both are Listed buildings and deserve analysis for their own merit. But there is a richer plausibility which is worth considering.

Writing in *Priory Demesne to University Campus, A topographical history of Nottingham University,* (1993), Frank Barnes tells us that the architect of Highfield House "was a Mr Wilkins, 'father of the late Venerable Archdeacon

Fig. 4

Highfield House
Architect: William Wilkins senior
1798

Fig. 5
*Donington Hall
Architect: William Wilkins senior
1790-1793*

Fig. 6
*Lenton Hall
(now Hugh Stewart Hall)
1792*

Wilkins' and architect to the Duke of Newcastle's estate". This was, as he later notes, William Wilkins the elder: no mention was made of the younger William Wilkins, the great Greek Revival scholar and architect of the National Gallery, and of University College, London, and Downing College, Cambridge. The father certainly was not as good an architect as the son, but he was not without interest.

What Frank Barnes does not tell us is that Lenton Hall could also be by William Wilkins senior. There is no evidence for this beyond the circumstantial. Indeed, Barnes says that it was built by William Stretton, whom he describes as "an accomplished artist with an eye for detail accurately observed, and a map maker, and he acted as surveyor for the Newcastle family", and he goes on to comment that "William Stretton became noted as an antiquarian." What Barnes does tell us is that a commendation applicable to William Wilkins' Donington Hall [5] - that it was one of the most correct specimens of true Gothic recently built - could equally well be applied to Lenton Hall [6]. But this is to rather over-estimate the quality of Lenton Hall. The Gothic (or rather Gothick) of neither Donington Hall nor, for that matter,

Lenton Hall, is particularly correct, and was soon recognised not to be, but that is here unimportant. Furthermore, Lenton Hall is a noticeably mean example of Gothick when compared to the much larger and infinitely more elaborate Donington Hall. What is important is that both Stretton and Wilkins appear to have worked for the Duke of Newcastle; that Wilkins is known to have built the adjacent property, Highfield House; that Stretton is not known to have built anything else in the fashionable Gothick style of Lenton Hall and Donington Hall, although he was styled a "surveyor" and a "builder"; and that Wilkins was introduced to Lord Moira of Donington Hall by Humphry Repton.

Humphry Repton, together with Lancelot "Capability" Brown, dominated English eighteenth century landscape design. In many ways their work was similar: the creation of a picturesque and apparently natural arcadia which was artificially contrived. But whereas Capability Brown's reputation is maintained by examples of his work, such as Stowe in Buckinghamshire, Repton's is retained in both his landscapes and his "Red Books". These were sketch books, bound in red leather for presentation to his clients, where the pages would show small and intimate sketches of views and aspects, before and after the great scheme was put into effect. And much of their success, and that of his landscapes, depended upon the disposition of the architecture, for which he needed an architect.

Initially, Repton used Wilkins as his architect. They were old friends, Wilkins one year the senior, and had grown up together in Norwich. Although Wilkins' family background was that of craftsmen plasterers - his grandfather had worked for Wren - Wilkins sought to better himself, and an association with

Humphry Repton, who could secure for him the appropriate introductions, provided just this opportunity. So from about 1785 to 1796, Humphry Repton and William Wilkins senior collaborated in a loose partnership, and from the early 1790s Wilkins took in Repton's son, John Adey Repton, as his pupil. It was only when the younger Repton completed his articles in 1796 and went to work as an assistant for John Nash, that the arrangement terminated. For now in Nash, Humphry Repton had a bigger fish to follow. Thus a game of social leapfrog led to the betterment of both parties.

Humphry Repton introduced William Wilkins to Lord Moira in 1789. The next year Wilkins prepared two plans and an elevation for Donington Hall. For this he was paid £21 in July 1790. Repton effected many introductions to estate-owners in the area which led directly or indirectly to commissions for Wilkins. There were gate houses at Babworth for John Bridgman Simpson (1790); work at Welbeck Abbey (1789) and extensions to Locko Park (1803) for the Duke of Portland; and gate lodges for Sir Henry Harpur at Calke Abbey (1804). And there might well be other buildings by Wilkins, although unrecorded, for Repton worked at Grove Hall (1790), Wingerworth (c.1791), and possibly Wansley Park (before 1795). Repton certainly visited Thoresby Hall, near Ollerton, home of Charles Pierrepont, later Earl Manvers and then first Viscount Newark, but it is not known whether he worked there, although a Red Book does survive. Nevertheless, Wilkins exhibited a "Design for improving the seat of a nobleman in Nottinghamshire" at the Royal Academy in 1799. This was probably Thoresby.

Although the architecture of Lenton Hall is similar to that of Donington Hall, it is not through this connection, for William

Fig. 7
*Lenton Hall gate lodge
1792*

Stretton *could* have worked in this style, but through the landscape that the argument that William Wilkins was the architect is best made. For the landscapes of Highfield House and Lenton Hall, together and separately, are quite Reptonian, and for the houses to be built so close together in both time and place, makes the circumstantial evidence very strong.

In 1794 Repton had drawn up a list of sixteen "Sources of Pleasure in Landscape Gardening". They included Utility, Order, Symmetry, Picturesque Effect, Simplicity, Variety, Contrast, Novelty, Association, Appropriation, Animation and the Seasons. Consequently the Reptonian landscape had a number of

recognisable features, many of which are still identifiable at Highfield House and Lenton Hall. Both houses are sited well so as to take advantage of the view, but neither does so at the cost of convenience. They both express a character equal to their social importance: Highfield House, the earlier of the two, is small, but is given a scale which renders it unmistakable for a farmhouse; Lenton Hall, built a few years later, sits on the ridge, its entrance front visible from the other side of the down, apparently lord of all it surveys. Both buildings are approached up long driveways and each from a single gate lodge [7], for paired gate lodges suggested, to Repton, forced symmetry: driveways, similarly, should not abut the road at right angles, but curve invitingly away. Cut Through Lane, the old approach to Highfield House runs uphill from a turn in Beeston Lane, its picturesque lodge once standing where Morley Horder's paired lodges do today; and Lenton Hall Drive still runs along the ridge towards Lenton Hall, although its junction with the Derby Road is less sweeping than it was before Lord Middleton, in a move to enlarge Wollaton Park, diverted the Nottingham to Derby Turnpike Road across Adams Hill in 1822. Both driveways, it can be imagined, would have offered dynamic, Reptonian views, through the trees, of the distant landscape: both driveways still do. Although the nature of the park which surrounded the two houses is now hard to discern, the static window-views which Repton advocated can, at least, be imagined from Highfield House, and surmised, in reverse, from early illustrations, while from Lenton Hall they can still be seen. Elsewhere, belts of planting remain, perhaps an echo of the early landscape, and trees still frame the views. But it is the lake which provides the most convincing suggestion of the Reptonian landscape. Far down below Highfield House and Lenton Hall, and fed by Tottle Brook which has wound its way from Wollaton, the lake, much smaller then than it is today, was the Reptonian masterpiece. Barnes quotes various 19th-century sales brochures which summarise the scene: "shrubbery walks and numerous rustic steps" lead to the lake "with islands and boathouse, surrounded by pretty and extensive woodland walks", the "massive rocks" forming "a novel feature of the place". An animated rusticity, rather than Capability Brown's smooth artificiality, was essential to the Reptonian lake. So Repton used deep bays and bold promontories, with lush waterside planting, to hold the eye. And the lake would be to the south, to catch the sun which would glitter from its moving surface, but not too close to the house, for glare would distract the eye from the middle distance, from the great Trent valley beyond.

Although William Wilkins senior did design Highfield House, there is, apparently, nothing beyond stylistic associations to say that he designed Lenton Hall as well. Pevsner gives the date of 1804 for Lenton Hall, the date also quoted, perhaps from Pevsner, by Barnes. But high on the south façade of Lenton Hall the date 1792 and the initials "DM" appear in the stonework. Although this is on the central bay rebuilt in 1905, it nevertheless raises the possibility that this building is in fact some years older than both Pevsner and Barnes suggest. And 1792 would make it exactly contemporaneous with Donington Hall, which Wilkins was building between 1790 and 1793, and four years before Wilkins' partnership with Humphry Repton ended. The similarity of the landscapes surrounding Lenton Hall and Highfield House suggests so strongly the influence, if not the hand of Repton, that both houses must surely be the work of one person: William Wilkins.

Highfield House

William Wilkin's design for Highfield House is simple to the point of plainness. One wonders what his son might have done with the same opportunity. The main house is four bays by three, two storeys tall with a simple overhanging cornice concealing a hidden gutter and the roof behind. The reordering of the house in 1928 has served to confuse the plan, but the principal east/west axial corridor, once leading from the main entrance, is still identifiable, with the stairs sweeping up in a gentle curve to one side and the dining room, an

Fig. 8

Highfield House
Architect: William Wilkins senior
1798

elegant, two-bay panelled room with acanthus mouldings in the cornice, to the other. In moving the entrance to the service court on the north side of the building, the 1928 alterations did away with the Grecian, pilastered entrance porch which marked the central bay of the west front and had served as a foil to the rather overscaled and detracting service wing to the side **[8]**. Although this west elevation is now imbalanced, the house still presents a fine south elevation, the balance between the subtly articulated bays, which identify the location of the dining room, and the positioning of the chimneys above allowing a breadth of dignity. The walls are stuccoed throughout, coursing lines marked with a trowel to suggest ashlar, and simple stuccoed architraves define the windows of the main house: the windows of the service wing remain undecorated.

Fig. 9
*Lenton Hall
(now Hugh Stewart Hall)
1792*

Lenton Hall

For all its plainness, there is a box-like solidity about Highfield House which is lacking in the paper-thin frivolity of Lenton Hall. Here is Gothick of the romantic, late-eighteenth century variety, wrapped around another Georgian box like mediaeval wallpaper. This is styling and an expression of fashion. As at William Wilkins' Donington Hall, there is no attempt to develop the romantic imagery with a picturesque outline, an irregular plan or an asymmetrical elevation. Lenton Hall is as four-square as Highfield House, but larger, seven bays by five, the bays being broader on the long fronts than on the end.

The thinness of the architecture is apparent in the battlements which encircle the building like a ruff, and the slender, polygonal corner turrets which breach the skyline and further partition the long façades. There is little of the strength of Caernarfon in this castle. The entrance porch on the north façade is a curious affair, more ecclesiastical than domestic, and almost believable were it not for the extraordinary octagonal corner turrets which rise like chimneys above the pierced tracery of the battlemented parapet **[9]**. The pointed arches' quadripartite vaulting appear insubstantial and the whole structure unnecessarily frail: but this was the fashion, for the Gothick was employed to

Fig. 10
*Lenton Hall
(now Hugh Stewart Hall)
1792
(central bay 1905)*

Fig. 11
*Lenton Grove
c.1825*

titillate and not, as did the Gothic Revival half a century later, to impart a message of morality. If Lenton Hall was indeed built in 1792, that would place it just six or seven years before Jane Austen wrote her Gothic novel *Northanger Abbey:* how Catherine Morland's heart might have palpitated at the sight of this Northanger Abbey!

With the Classical sense of balance and symmetry which belies the styling of this building, the garden elevation to the south would have reflected almost exactly (with the omission of the porch) the elevation to the north. But this façade was remodelled in 1905 for George Cresswell Bond, the entrance hall and the central bay of the building being rebuilt with more than a dash of the Baroque thrown in [10]. The result, at least in as much as it affects the south elevation, is quite incongruous. The new central bay, which provides french doors to the garden, steps forward with a great, half-broken segmental pediment, heavy dentils, an oversized and penetrating

keystone, a shouldered architrave and two engaged Ionic columns: an architecture quite alien to its context. Above, as if to echo the heave of the Baroque pediment, a new cusped and pinnacled "Jacobethan" pediment, suggested perhaps by Wollaton Hall, breaks the skyline. Up here in the blocking course is that intriguing date 1792, and also the date 1905, a year which is repeated in the "Jacobethan" hopper heads on the west elevation.

The Lenton Park Estate

Although some of the Lenton Park estates were developed at the start of the nineteenth century, the middle years of the century are largely unrepresented, the final subdivision of the lands not occurring until towards the end of the century. What remains of a late Georgian house can be detected in the white stuccoed and slate-roofed rear portions of Lenton Firs, more recently called Wortley Hall, and a similar but more complete architecture is apparent down the hill at Lenton Grove and Lenton Fields House.

Lenton Grove and Lenton Fields House

Lenton Grove (c. 1825) [11] and Lenton Fields House (c. 1837) [12] represent, in a modest way, the two fashionable modes of late-Georgian and Williamene domestic architecture: the Tuscan villa and the Palladian styles. Although now Listed buildings, both houses have undergone such extensive remodelling that the signifying characteristics of the originals are hard to recognise. In Lenton Grove, the original T-shaped plan can be identified in the positioning of the entrance and the gracious, curving, top-lit stairs, even if it is lost externally. The overhanging eaves, such a feature of Tuscan villas, still remain. At Lenton Fields House, the boxiness of the original two-storey, stuccoed villa remains, but the chimneys, which must have provided some counterpoint to the heavily horizontal cornice and blocking course, have been removed. Polygonal and semi-circular bay windows, both nineteenth-century additions, extend rather unhappily from flanking windows on the east and west fronts but do not look nearly so ridiculous as the new "Doric", flat roofed entrance portico gracing the central bay of the front elevation. A rap of the knuckles on the paired columns, which betray no sign of entasis, immediately proves them to be plastic, perhaps, or glass fibre, and *this* in a Listed building!

Fig. 12
Lenton Fields House c.1837

Fig. 13
*Lenton Eaves
1875*

Lenton Eaves

The one stylistically mid-nineteenth century house is Lenton Eaves **[13]**, built up against the Derby Road for Benjamin Walker, principal of the lace makers, Benjamin Walker and Co., in 1875. But as an example of contemporary architecture it is disappointing, for it draws neither upon the fashionable Gothic nor the newly introduced Old English and Queen Anne styles. Rather it adopts the boxiness of a Georgian villa and the picturesque details of a shooting lodge or even a rural railway station. Although pointed gables, gablets and canopies abound, the window and door openings remain resolutely square-headed, their shouldered and chamfered lintels set uncompromisingly in stone against the red brickwork of the walls. The eaves overhang in the Tuscan manner and are supported by decorated timber trusses with open, trefoil-headed tracery. Brick corbels, machicolations, string courses and banding abound and, with the assistance of square and polygonal bay windows, serve to disguise the boxiness of the building. Most convincing, perhaps, is the double-light, trefoil-headed, plate tracery of the tall stair window but even this lacks conviction, for inside it is framed in timber. Timber, too, is the square newel stair, a curious confection of Gothic motifs incorporating engaged shafts on the newel posts, turned balusters on the treads, and stiff-leaf decoration. It is done with verve but little comprehension. As an example of copybook Gothic, Lenton Eaves is interesting, but whether used by an architect or a jobbing builder, this particular copy-book was certainly not new.

Fig. 14
Lenton Firs
Background: Georgian villa
Middle ground: Stables
Architect: Thomas C Hine 1862
Foreground: Coachman's house
Architect: Evans and Sons 1904

Lenton Firs

The Georgian villa, Lenton Firs, had received a new Gothic gate lodge, to the design of Thomas C Hine, in 1862. At that time the house was modernised, presumably by Hine, and the front rooms, stairs and arcaded hallway, as used today, were added. So too was the stable block at the rear [14]. The house was further modernised by the architects Evans and Jolley for William Lambert of W J and T Lambert, bleachers, dyers and lace makers, in 1888. It is likely that Robert Evans got the commission because he had been articled to T C Hine: his partner, William Jolley, had worked for Sir Gilbert Scott. The drawings, which are dated 2 December 1887, indicate the refacing of the south and east fronts of the house in brick and half timbering [15], the addition of two-storey window bays flanking a new front entrance porch, and the rebuilding of the rear entrance. The interior arrangement, apparently, changed little, the drawing room and library overlooking the front lawns and the dining room with billiard room beyond, to the side. The house was purchased by Sir Thomas Shipstone, the brewer, in 1903 and it was he who installed the stained glass which is such a feature of the entrance hall, stairs and landing, and he also who, in 1904, rebuilt the stables and added a coachman's house on the north side. His architects were the same firm, but now called Evans and Sons, and the style was the same, Old English, and in keeping.

Fig. 15
Lenton Firs
Architect: Evans and Jolley
1887

West Hill House

In 1881, six years before working on Lenton Firs, Evans and Jolley had designed a house for an adjacent plot to the other side of Lenton Hall Drive. This was to be West Hill House [16], later known as the Cedars (from 1905) and now Paton House (from 1948). Built for Samuel Herrick Sands, JP, it lacks the stylishness of Lenton Firs, but there Evans and Jolley had been given a good lead by T C Hine. The north entrance front of West Hill House is drab and uninviting, the canopied and balustered porch heavy and incongruous against the flat gables of the façade. The south front to the garden, which was probably as severe as the north front, is now more varied and interesting due to addition of a pair of matching gables and bay windows, built in brick with stone trimmings, hung tiles and timber corbels. Similarly, the development, into a conservatory, of the slender, sheltered verandah opening off the library, gives the west elevation a touch of lightness.

Internally, much of the building has been institutionalised, but vestiges of a greater elegance remain in the panelled screen wall to the entrance hall and the pilastered, Baroque interior of what would have been the dining room, behind the later bay windows of the south front.

Fig. 16
*West Hill House
Architect: Evans and Jolley
1881*

Fig. 17
Redcourt
Architect: Martin and Hardy
1882

Redcourt

Some six years before William Lambert rebuilt Lenton Firs, his brother John Lambert had instructed architects Martin and Hardy to build a house on the plot to the west of West Hill House. This was to be Redcourt, a large and rather heavy house in the fashionable Old English style, characterised by the use of red brick and tile, tall Tudor chimneys, stone window trimmings and half timbering [17]. The drawings, dated 24 March 1882, show an apparently prosperous and well-appointed family house with a library, billiard room and nursery, and one bathroom, two water closets (one family's and one house maids') and one earth closet, presumably for the ground staff. Yet stylistically it is unconvincing. The garden front is appropriately asymmetrical, the larger window bay accommodating the drawing room and the other, to the east, the dining room. But the constant, unbroken lines of the ridge and the coved eaves reduce the picturesque effect so much so that the single, off-centred chimney just looks out of place. The large, half-timbered bay to the west which accommodates the library and, above that, the nursery, redeems that elevation somewhat but all is lost on the north, entrance front where the handling of tall, expressed chimney stacks, half-timbered gables and dormer windows is simply inarticulate. The more recent rebuilding of the entrance as a white, flat-roofed porch has destroyed anything which that façade might have had to offer.

Fig. 18
Lenton Hurst
Architect: Marshall and Turner
1896

Lenton Hurst

The aspirations and shortcomings of these various villas are worth considering for they serve to highlight the undoubted success of the last of the grand suburban houses to be built along the Derby Road boundary of the Lenton Park estates. This was the house built for W G Player, the cigarette manufacturer, by architects Marshall and Turner in 1896, and was called Lenton Hurst [18]. Arthur Marshall was a good architect, clearly a cut above Messrs Evans and Jolley, and Martin and Hardy. He was born in Nottingham in 1858 (died 1915) and articled to the antiquarian and architect Samuel Dutton Walker, whose name still lives on in an annual prize awarded in the School of Architecture. Marshall was an accomplished draughtsman, as his published work shows, an amateur photographer and President of the Nottingham Camera Club, and, in 1901-02, President of the Nottingham Architectural Society. He was an expert in infirmary and workhouse architecture, and the designer of St Augustine's RC Church in Nottingham. In 1888 he published a bound folio of drawings called *Specimens of Carved Antique Furniture and Woodwork*, dedicated to Princess Louise, Marchioness of Lorne. It was well received: "The book is one of the best of its kind," wrote *The Builder,* although, in considering the Old Settle at Retford, it noted that "There is ... something rather coarse and barbaric about the style of this work."

Nevertheless, it was *this* style of work, and the architect's eye for the topical if not the most innovative, which gave

Fig. 19
The Hallams, Surrey
Architect:
Richard Norman Shaw
1896

Fig. 20
Lenton Hurst
Architect: Marshall and Turner
1896

Lenton Hurst its edge. For this building uses its site in a dramatic and imaginative way, which both West Hill House and Redcourt failed to do, and succeeds in being both articulate in its arrangement and informed in its detailing. And for this, Arthur Marshall surely owes more than a little to Richard Norman Shaw.

It was Norman Shaw who can be largely credited with popularising the Old English style. He had begun using it in the late 1860s and his drawings were regularly hung at the Royal Academy and illustrated in the architectural press. Although his use of the style was usually confined to the Home Counties, he did take it further afield and sometimes employed it in non-domestic situations where it would have been more accessible to the casual visitor. Sprout Hall, built in Leek, Staffordshire, in 1871-73, was one such example. It is feasible that Arthur Marshall had seen this building: the research for his book on *Carved Antique Furniture and Wood-work* certainly took him far afield. But by 1896, when Marshall designed Lenton Hurst for W G Player, the Old English Style was anything but new: indeed, it had been around for almost thirty years. So Marshall's effort could be dismissed for being largely outdated were it not for the fact that Norman Shaw's last house in the style, a convincing example called The Hallams at Shamley Green, Surrey, was published in *The Building News* on 3 January that year [19]. Marshall dated his drawings five months later, on 4 June 1896 [20].

Lenton Hurst sits to the west of Redcourt, just where the ground falls away towards Lenton Eaves, its situation amplified by the rockeries and sunken garden to the south and west, which might have resulted from the quarrying of building stone. Thus it appears to rise out of the very ground from which it came. What is essentially an L-shaped plan is focused about this south-west corner, where the roofs and chimneys collide in a crescendo of half-timbered gables, tile hanging and Tudor brickwork. From here the south front stretches away, from drawing room to morning room to dining room and kitchen, a series of chimneys and gables, a low pair at the end providing a counterpoint to the huge gable on the corner. The west front is similarly gabled, but now the roof drops down as a counter-balance to the sturdiness of the battlemented, stone tower, which terminates this façade. Strong and masculine, it signifies the men's domains and the presence of the billiard room. By arranging the building around this corner Marshall manages the composition supremely well and retains the full picturesque effect. And here he makes the most obvious reference to The Hallams, for the tall, Tudor brick chimney stack is stepped, shafted and stone-splattered just as the one in Shaw's published perspective.

The north front of Lenton Hurst is a vibrant composition of irregular parts expressed in brick, stone and hung tile [21]. A bellcote, barely visible from the garden front, rises above the great stair window, a Norman Shaw touch suggestive of what could be another but more distant source for this house: Pierrepont at Frensham, Surrey, built in 1876-78, exhibited at the Royal Academy in 1876 and published in *The Building News* on 25 May that year. To one side, symmetry is boldly suggested in the paired, half-timbered gables and central chimney and rainwater pipe of the west wing, only to be denied by the irregularly placed upper windows and the quirky, square corner oriel overlooking the entrance. The porch itself is a long,

Fig. 21

Lenton Hurst
architect: Marshall and Turner
1896

tunnel-vaulted, pargetted and strap-worked affair set beneath a protruding, pitched roof and oversailing, "Jacobethan" canopy supported on Ionic corbel brackets. Here perhaps is the influence of Marshall's book on *Carved Antique Furniture and Woodwork:* yet the intention of the book was not that of a copy-book, but rather a record of late mediaeval and early renaissance work **[22]**. As he wrote in the introduction:

It is my desire to enlist, as far as possible, the sympathies of the public in favour of an

art, which has been somewhat inadequately treated in English literature in the past, that the better acquainted the public becomes with this art, the more appreciative they will be of its merits, and the more sympathy they will show with the efforts of those workers of old, whose ambitions it was to produce works of such utility and beauty.

Internally, the plan of Lenton Hurst draws from The Hallams as well. Shaw's published drawing showed a fairly standard L-shaped arrangement, with drawing room, library and dining room

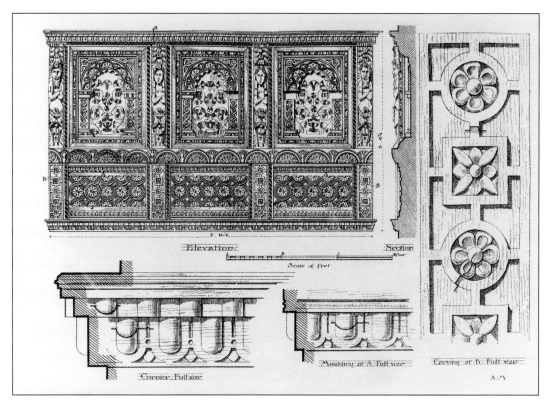

making up the garden range, and the billiard room located mid-way along the other arm. Much of this Marshall re-employs, departing only from Shaw's general strategy in positioning the billiard room at the end of the west wing, and thus flanking the front door, and by reinterpreting Shaw's octagonal bay from the main hall as the rounded bay of the billiard room. But more significant, for its uniqueness and precision, is the treatment of the entranceway which Shaw uses to separate the square newel stair from the main hall, and then further separates from the main hall by an arcaded screen. This Marshall duplicates.

It is in the entranceway and main hall that Marshall's own specialist knowledge comes to the fore. The walls are panelled in oak and the ceiling shows floor joists and the exposed, underside of floor-boards: it is, as *The Builder* suggested of the Old Settle at Retford, "something rather coarse and barbaric", but it is intentional. There is greater and expected sophistication in the arcaded screen with its dogtooth moulding and ornamental strapwork; in the square newel staircase with its turned balusters and strapworked strings; in the plastered, strapwork ceiling above the stairs with its pendentives, perhaps once intended for lights but now broken off; and in the upper landing where an elegant balustered screen contained between Tuscan columns hides the stairs to the upper floor. The centrepiece of Marshall's work is the fireplace in the main hall, a "Jacobethan" composition incorporating engaged Ionic columns and a high mantelpiece, side-lit from a square bay window alcove flanked by oak settles **[23]**. In *Specimens of Carved Antique Furniture and Woodwork* he wrote:

It was understood by the old architects that few features were more necessary in an apartment than a well designed chimney piece and overmantel. The best examples of the carving of the period with which we are dealing are generally to be found in the fireplaces and overmantels, where, as a rule, the greater part of the ornamental work of a room was centred.

and Woodwork, but is more akin to one included in *The Builder* on 14 April 1888, the week following the published review of the book. This illustration shows the Jacobean chimneypiece in Holdenby House, Northamptonshire, which was being restored at just this time by R H Carpenter, and incorporates framed oak panels set beneath a high mantel supported on a pair of Tuscan columns. Yet the proportions are different from that at Lenton Hurst, as is the choice of Order.

Fig. 23
*Lenton Hurst Main Hall
rchitect: Marshall and Turner
1896*

Surprisingly, this design is not drawn from any fireplaces illustrated in *Specimens of Carved Antique Furniture*

Chapter 3

Morley Horder and the Highfields Site

Morley Horder

In 1887, when he was sixteen or seventeen years old, Percy Morley Horder had written to the great architectural critic, John Ruskin, then an old man living at Brantwood, near Coniston in the Lake District, requesting advice on his proposed career in architecture. "My dear boy", Ruskin had replied in an avuncular way, "There is one book on architecture of any value - and that contains everything, rightly. Mons' Viollet le Duc's Dictionary. Every architect must learn French for all the best architecture is in France - and the French workmen are in the highest degree skilful. For the rest, you must trust your own feeling & observation only. My books are historical & sentimental and very well in their way. But you must learn from the things themselves." This advice was given in March 1887 and was appropriate, for it recommended the Arts and Crafts philosophy current at the time. In the event, Percy Morley Horder took up articles with George Devey, where Charles F A Voysey had recently worked (1880-81), and thus entered into a world of folksy vernacular and cottagey imagery representative of, yet not central to, the Arts and Crafts Movement.

Although this would seem an unlikely background for the architect of a new University College, it was symptomatic of the times. Many were the Arts and Crafts architects who, after the Great War, changed their coat to one of a grander, more Classical appearance: F W Troup, the designer of a model cottage at Letchworth (1905) and consultant architect to the Bank of England (from 1921) was one; Sir Edwin Lutyens was another. Morley Horder's route was more obviously commercial, one of his clients being also the benefactor of the new University College, Sir Jesse Boot.

During the latter years of the War, Morley Horder built or fitted out a number of shops for Boots Cash Chemists: at Bristol in 1916-17, at Eastbourne in 1917, and at Windsor in 1918-19, as well as shops in Lincoln, Brighton and Regent Street, London. Boots Cash Chemists were not the pharmaceutical retailers known today, but rather a complex of toilet specialists, dispensing chemists, cafe and smoking room. The style Morley Horder employed was classical but of a domestic scale, Edwardian Georgian. As his obituary in the *RIBA Journal* in 1944 noted, "Morley Horder was one of the now diminishing band of architects who carried the Morris tradition into its aristocratic Edwardian phase."

Why Sir Jesse Boot should commission his own commercial architect to design the new University College is uncertain: perhaps he was the architect Boot knew best. Morley Horder was, by all accounts, "popularly reckoned an eccentric and he was reputed difficult stuff for clients to deal with but however much this may have been true, for those who had the pleasure of his friendship he could be the most engaging and stimulating conversationalist and correspondent with an alert and critical awareness of happenings and opinion." It could be that for Boot, as a businessman, it was just a matter of expediency, for *The Builder* described Morley Horder as "a sound, practical architect": alternatively, there might have been a common understanding between these two unusual men. Following the publication of Morley Horder's obituary in the *RIBA Journal,* Sir Herbert Baker wrote that "his brother Gerald used to say that as he himself suffered from an inferiority complex, his brother Morley suffered from a superiority complex."

Morley Horder was not such an unlikely choice for a new University College as might be thought. He had won the competition, judged by Sir Aston Webb, for the Cheshunt Congregational College in Cambridge, built between 1913 and 1915. Although Tudor and quadrangular, and very different from what he was to build at Highfields, the design did suggest an understanding of traditional collegiate architecture. Contemporary also with the new University College was his building of the London School of Hygiene and Tropical Medicine in Gower Street, designed in partnership with Verner O Rees and later described as "one of the most successful designs in Portland stone since Hawksmoor and Vanbrugh". There is a distinct similarity, in both plan and elevation, between these two buildings, evidence, perhaps, as the *RIBA Journal* noted in another context, of "his careful academicism getting the upperhand."

The notion to build a new University at Highfields had come to Sir Jesse Boot in the summer of 1921. The original intent had been to use the land for a model village to provide accommodation for his factory workers: the University was to be located on the river near Trent Bridge, south of the Meadows. But the United Drug Company of America, to whom he had sold controlling rights in his Pure Drug Company in 1919, would not back the scheme and so Boot, apparently as the result of a chance remark made to him while viewing the Highfields Estate one day, resolved to locate his university there. Plans proceeded apace, and in June 1922, the new University College was founded by Lord Haldane of Cloan.

Fig. 24
Trent Building
Architect: P Morley Horder
1928

The New University College

The building which King George V and Queen Mary opened at Highfields on 10 July 1928 was received, by the architectural press, with almost universal acclaim [24]. The reviews published over the following weeks were surprisingly uncritical, with references to "the 'genius' of the architect" being not uncommon. "The architect, Mr P Morley Horder," wrote *The Architects' Journal*, "has been extremely ingenious in solving a number of difficult problems." At a dinner held that evening to celebrate the event, it was made clear that Jesse Boot had been very much involved with the development of the design, and this the journals duly reported: "The layout of the plans, the design of the buildings, and, in fact, almost every detail, had passed through the brain of Sir Jesse Boot, who has given half a million

Fig. 25
*Trent Building
Architect: P Morley Horder
1928*

Fig. 26
*Trent Building
Architect: P Morley Horder
1928*

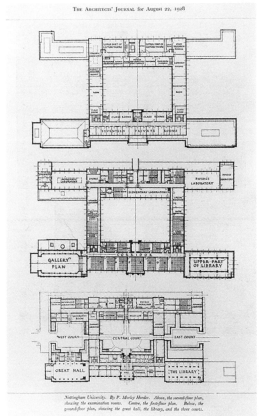

pounds towards Nottingham's future University, and, we are informed, has suggested many of the plans to the architect, who has provided the dignified buildings, specially adapted for the modern needs of higher education, and suitable to a very beautiful site." What was clear, was that the industrial background of the patron was instrumental in the developing of a modern university which was reflected in the programme for the buildings. "Sir Jesse Boot, to whose munificence both park and buildings are due, is inspired with the desire that modern science should be studied in all its branches in order to serve British industry, and for that reason the architect has had to design a number of laboratories of various kinds."

Described as "dignified, even severe, at first sight" **[25]**, the new University College was arranged around a square court **[26]**, with wings extending to east

Fig. 27
*Trent Building
Architect: P Morley Horder
1928*

somewhat small, but this is intentional, for it signifies the academic building. The man should be humble in the face of the search for knowledge" [27]. If there was an academic provenance for this elevation, it most probably was in the work of Sir Aston Webb, Morley Horder's champion in the Cheshunt Congregational College competition, for Webb's Royal Naval College at Dartmouth provides two clues as to the design of the front block at the new University College. The first is in the *partis* of Webb's original building of 1899-1905, a long, thin elevation, with the two major spaces, the chapel and the dining hall, placed one at each end and connected by an uninterrupted corridor over 450ft (135m) in length [28]. The effect is extraordinary, for the arrangement is so perfectly axial that from the altar steps a view can be obtained right through to the dining hall and even to the servery, kitchen and scullery beyond. This was repeated at Nottingham with the Great Hall and the Library as the terminal features, but neither was set quite on axis, as Webb had done, and the effect was thus lost. The second clue is in the elevation of Webb's extension to the Royal Naval College known as "D Block" which was exhibited at the Royal Academy and published in *The British Architect* in 1916 [29]. This building reflected the arrangement of the first but now with a plan more suggestive of one side of a square court with wings extending to east and west. It is a long and severe elevation, raised up and overlooking a terrace, its central feature, as at Nottingham, being a weak portico with its pediment set within the blocking course.

The Nottingham plan, as has been noted, was re-employed at the London School of Hygiene and Tropical Medicine [30]. The central court provided the

and west, and presented a broad elevation to the south, over 400ft (120m) long, in a style which, according to *The Builder,* suggested Vignola. Another weekly, *The Architects' Journal* commented that "the principal building is not unduly imposing, for it is meant to show at the outset that the building is designed for hard work on the part of the staff and the students, and not for ostentation." This interpretation must have been put forward, perhaps by the University or Boot's spokesman, in a press release or an after-dinner speech, for it is picked up again by *The Builder:* "There are only two columns on the whole front, suggesting the ceremonial nature of the central entrance. The entrance is

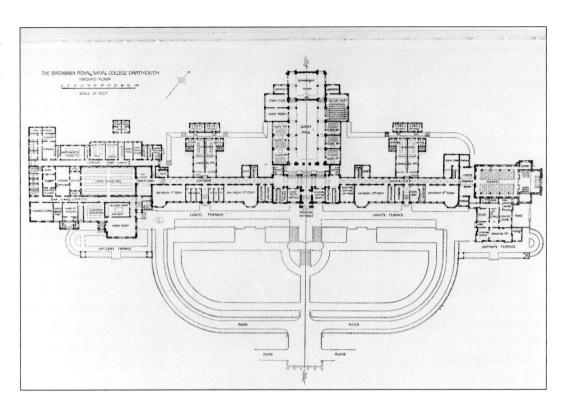

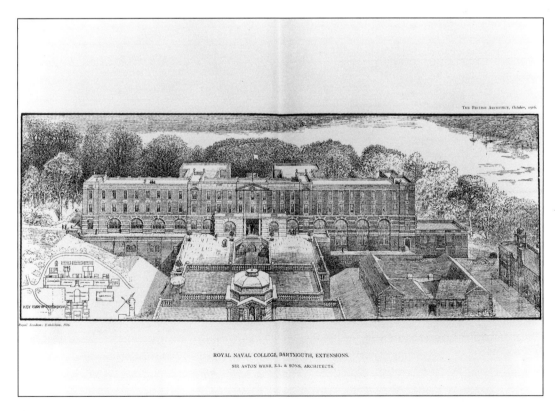

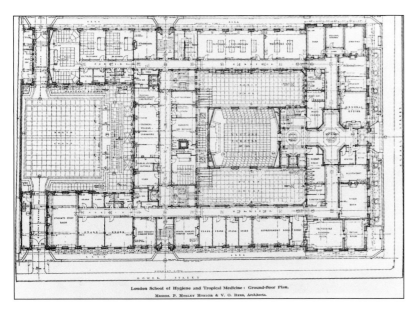

Fig. 30
London School of Hygiene and
Tropical Medicine
Architect: P Morley Horder
(designed 1926)

possibility for axial (in London) and cross-axial access (in Nottingham), with circulation by a cloister-like corridor which flanked the central court on two sides but was contained between rows of parallel rooms on the other two: the stairs were located in the corners. Where the London plan really differs from that at Nottingham is that the central court contains a large lecture theatre, an exigency of the urban site which the rural location of the Nottingham building rendered unnecessary. But if using a rural plan-type on an urban site created problems of accommodation, using an urban plan-type on a rural site created problems of elevation. The plain Portland stone and simplified classical decoration of the London School of Hygiene and Tropical Medicine provides a foil to the stock brick and stucco trim of Gower Street, a large building in a street of smaller parts. At Nottingham, Morley Horder had no nearby buildings to respond to, his context being purely rural. Yet he chose again Portland stone and adopted a stripped classicism even more severe than at Gower Street. The only articulation which he allowed the main elevation was in the forwards/backwards

rhythm of the bays, 7-7-3-7-7, the central distyle-in-antis portico surprisingly slight against the length of that façade, its pediment restrained beneath the roofline. So as if to remedy this weakness, he added the tower, the one feature of which the reviews were critical.

The tower was Italianate, a Tuscan villa campanile set against the Nottinghamshire downs. *The Architects' Journal* noted that it had been "criticised in some quarters as being too light, and not in harmony with the masses of the main building." *The Builder* similarly commented that "above the main entrance stands the tower that has been criticised in some places, but it should be noticed", it added, "that this is simply a bell tower, and without it the whole building would certainly be very flat and plain." It was *The Architect and Building News* which took it most seriously, its account of the new building appearing under the title "Nottingham University College. The use of a tower as an Architectural Symbol". It argued that the tower, as an architectural symbol of social import-ance, was well-suited to a university building, and economical to build, but commented that "there are not many instances, however, in which a tall tower of narrow base is made the central feature of an architectural composition as much as 400ft. from side to side." By comparison, it was thought that the tower worked well enough when viewed from within the central court: "Its base as seen from the north elevation is well articulated and is studiously kept in scale with the façade of the court. The super-structure shows a decorative treatment by which the sides of the tower are sub-divided by means of balconies, and small pediments surmounting the clock faces, while the whole is crowned by a low-pitched roof with weather vane." The problem, really, is that the tower is misplaced. Through its slightness, it gives nothing to the south façade, and being centrally placed, it halves that long horizontal with a weak vertical line. Morley Horder would have done better to dispense with the tower, or relocate it on the opposite side of the court, and provide the south elevation with a good deal more punch.

Internally, the new University College was well thought-out and clearly arranged. At either end of the main façade, a double-height Library balanced the double-height Great Hall, with administrative offices and the Council Chamber in-between. Classrooms and offices were accommodated on the upper floors and extended as far back as the east/west axis, beyond which line laboratories and lecture rooms took over, the sciences effectively separated from the arts. Here there were elementary laboratories and advanced laboratories and a room for special research; there were designated laboratories for maths, physics, chemistry and pharmacy, for professors and for research; there were rooms for physical chemistry, and for organic chemistry, for gas analysis and for bacteria medica; and there was a workshop, two museums and a geography room. "Experts of academic buildings who visited Nottingham last Tuesday", wrote *The Builder,* "were full of praise for the well-lighted lecture rooms and laboratories." If there was any common ground between what C P Snow called "the two cultures", it was in the examination rooms which were located on the top floor above the dividing axis. As *The Architects' Journal* had observed, "Mr Morley Horder recognised, too, from the outset that he was building a modern university, and not an imitation of a mediaeval university. . . where science will be called upon to the full to help on a local industry. Thus the scientific needs

had to be fully considered. The essential success of the design lies in the fact that it expresses so well the ideas that inspired its generous founder."

Despite the highly specific nature of the plan, the new University College was intended to be a flexible building, and so had lightweight partitions which could be easily removed: "In short, the interior is elastic to suit modern requirements." Rich materials were retained for only the permanent spaces. The main corridor was lined in black Belgian marble, and the loggia with Hopton Wood marble, while the Council Chamber was panelled in oak and the Dining Hall, set beneath the Library, was finished in Roman marble and provided with oak screens at either end. The Great Hall, which could seat 750, was allowed a degree of theatricality, "the columns on each side suggest Egypt rather than an industrial city", which *The Architects' Journal* thought "possibly a little incongruous with the distinctively English simplicity of the whole building." Beneath the Great Hall was the Lower Hall, large enough to accommodate 450 and with a sprung floor for dancing. "Both halls", *The Architects' Journal* noted, "are unexpectedly unacademic. One London professor at the opening remarked of the Great Hall that it was reminiscent of a picture palace *de luxe.* This may be intentional, as it will be used a great deal for the music and drama." A more academic atmosphere was found in the galleried Library, with its scagliola columns and its niches containing alabaster busts of wise men of the east.

The new University College became the Trent Building in 1953. In losing its name, it also lost its original function and thus its identity. No longer was it *the* University building, but one amongst many. As a compact yet flexible design containing all the functions of an academic establishment, the new University College had probably worked very well. In its axial arrangement, the symmetry of the plan imparted dignity to the new edifice as well as reflecting the bipartite nature of the two cultures. In its formal arrangement it dominated its site but allowed no space or opportunity for expansion. So when its science departments decamped to new buildings down the hill, the integrity of the plan was compromised, and when the Portland Building was built just along the hillside, its position was challenged and its dominance of the site was lost.

The Entrance Buildings

The positioning of the new University College on high ground above the lake provided Morley Horder with the opportunity for a long, axial approach from the new University Boulevard, laid

out by the engineer W H Radford, in 1921. The fact that this axis strikes straight through the lake, thus rendering the route inaccessible, is ignored. For at the south end of the route, up against the Boulevard, Morley Horder erected an entrance way of two low, curved screen walls incorporating lodges. Built of Darley stone, darker and more dignified than the bright Portland stone of the College building on the escarpment above, the entrance is of a reserved classicism, enhanced by two richly swagged, Vanbrugh-esque oval windows, one on either side. In reality this entrance did not provide access to the University, but rather to the pleasure grounds surrounding the lake, which remained the property of the Corporation, and an axial connection with the University's playing fields located on the south side of University Boulevard. Access to the campus was through the

Fig. 31
Lido
Architect: P Morley Horder
1924

south gate, located further along University Boulevard, and by the west gate off Beeston Lane.

The development of the City Corporation's pleasure grounds preceded the building of the University College. The excavation required for the enlargement of the lake provided material for the embankment of University Boulevard as well as for the foundations of the new College building, and the lake itself, fed from Tottle Brook, provided the water for the Lido. Here, on the lake, leisure and learning, and town and gown, could come together, overlooked from one end by the Corporation's Tea Pavilion, and from the other by the new University College.

Opened in August 1924, Morley Horder's Lido **[31]**, which in its time was the largest inland swimming pool in Britain (measuring 330 x 75ft or 99 x 22.5m), was the first part of the development to be completed. The buildings, which incorporated 252 changing cubicles, were of brick and in the Tuscan style of the Italian *campagna:* rounded arches in loggia, pitched roofs and parapet walls, overhanging eaves and a small belvedere. In keeping with its scale, it had three steel-framed diving structures comprising two chutes and one three-tier diving board. There was also a low springboard.

On an axis perpendicular to the Lido was the Tea Pavilion, also by Morley Horder and also Italianate. Originally intended as a ballroom and restaurant, it was completed by 1928, but soon became a gymnasium once the College opened. Built of brick, it is a T-shaped building, the principal axis tying in the Lido on one side with the lake on the other. The cross axis picks up the pedestrian entrance from University Boulevard and would

have continued up the downs on the other side: today it terminates, most fortuitously, with the tall campus chimney, but whether this is by chance or design is hard to say. Facing the Lido, on the principal axis, is a central, half-domed alcove providing, beneath overhanging eaves, an open-air stage flanked by niches: at the top of the T, facing the lake, an open, colonnaded court once provided the perfect ambience for an afternoon tea overlooking the rowing boats. Here, where wrought iron balconies extend beyond the grand sweep of the embankment wall with its giant, stone planters, there is a sense of confidence and prosperity. Parapet urns and *bas* reliefs depicting lutes and trumpets, wildlife and wildfowl, suggest the dignity and cultural aspirations of this place as well as its outdoor ethos. Here flappers and blue-stockings alike could take tea and tango.

Across on the other side of the Highfields site, the west gate lodges **[32]** marked the original campus entrance from Beeston Lane. Built where the *ornée* gate lodge to Highfield House once stood, they are now isolated, as if by a receding tide, within the campus grounds. Old photographs show these two lodges flanking that *cottage ornée* before it was demolished, a curious juxtaposition. The west gate lodges, designed by Morley Horder, are identical, square, two-storey Darley stone boxes with a pediment to each façade, Ionic yet astylar. As neat, classical essays, they would have prepared the visitor for the gated academicism of the new community, something the more recent gateway building at the south entrance fails to do. But the gates have gone, removed when Beeston Lane was widened, to be replaced by sensors and a security box further down the road.

Fig. 32
*West Gate Lodges
Architect: P Morley Horder
1928*

The First Halls of Residence

The removal of the University College from Shakespeare Street to Highfields in 1928 created a problem in terms of student accommodation. The four existing halls, two for men and two for women, were situated near the Arboretum and further afield, in Mapperley Park and Sherwood. Convenient, to a degree, for Shakespeare Street, they were a long haul from Highfields. So in 1928 the first accommodation on the new campus was built. This was a hall for women and named after Florence Boot, its benefactrix and Sir Jesse's wife [33]. Morley Horder was again the architect although here his approach was far more homely and domestic than at the new University College building or at Hugh Stewart Hall: here he was the Arts and Crafts architect, the architect who built a house for David Lloyd George at Walton Heath, Surrey. Yet Pevsner describes the building as "dreary neo-Georgian" and "of no special merit." It is a description which, although not altogether unwarranted, is perhaps rather hastily made, for Florence Boot Hall deserves some consideration.

Florence Boot Hall employs an H-shaped plan, with recreational and service rooms on the ground floor and study bedrooms above. The students' rooms are arranged on corridors rather than staircases, setting a precedent which was followed in the later halls on campus and which encouraged one critic writing in *The Architects' Journal* in 1960 to comment:

All the men's halls have been designed on the courtyard principle, with staircases giving access to the study bedrooms. This apparently vital principle of university design, however, is not applied in the case of the women's hostel to the east of the Park,

Fig. 33
*Florence Boot Hall
Architect: P Morley Horder
1928*

which has been planned on the corridor system, in accordance, presumably, with the traditional, institutional character of buildings for women.

The feeling of Florence Boot Hall is that of a large country house, perhaps, or of a hotel. Its use of brick distinguishes it from the new, stone-built buildings higher up the hill: an analogy can be drawn here to Newnham College, Cambridge, where Basil Champneys used the new Queen Anne Revival style in 1875 to distinguish this, the first ladies' college, from those gothic and classical buildings previously built for men. As a result, Florence Boot Hall is not particularly institutional and certainly not academic, the "quadrangle" to the rear appearing more like a lawn surrounded by tea terraces. Yet the front elevation is too tall for the restricted space it commands, its three storeys of casement

and sash windows arranged in a 2-5-2 rhythm, solid and symmetrical, with a low, distyle doric entrance portico smack in the middle. From here an axial procession should develop, but it fails to, for the blank, back wall of the library blocks the route through and diverts the visitor along corridors to the left or the right, without indication of where or why. It is the same entry sequence as Horder used at the University College building, and as unsatisfactory. Nevertheless, the entrance negotiated, the visitor will find the junior common room in the east wing, to the left, and the dining room in the west, to the right, both pleasant and spacious rooms with fanlight french doors opening through arcaded walls to either side. When first furnished with rattan chairs, the junior common room must have had the feeling of a seaside hotel at Brighton or Torquay: in the opposite wing, the dining room extension of 1959 - a five-bay arcade overlooking a possible parterre - has all the qualities of an orangery.

Yet many of the internal features are more robust, even masculine. The stairs, both square newel and straight flights, are worked in oak with a truly Arts and Crafts feel - simple, square-lattice balustrades and strong newel posts suggestive of Edwardian country houses in the home counties: elsewhere, radiators are hidden behind open grilles and study bedrooms behind simply panelled doors, and all in oak. It is a finish rather at odds with the atmosphere of the place, but reassuring and homely. It is a quality recreated more recently in the bar, a facility Florence Boot would never have condoned, where sympathetic oak panelling and an unexpected apsidal conservatory, steel and *prêt à porter,* make for a rather special place. Strangely, the conservatory faces north.

In what is generally a featureless building of pale brick and concrete sills, Horder reserves his decoration for the three elevations facing the garden court to the rear. Here niches with stone planting boxes are inserted between the arcaded openings of the five french doors on each façade, the three central windows of each arcade surmounted by small, cast iron balconies at first floor level. In a balanced and symmetrical space, the only inconsistency being the protruding bay window of the senior common room: perhaps an addition. And that, excluding the stone-coped parapets and shallow mansards behind, is just about it.

Horder certainly did not leave F S Eales many useful leads to follow when extending the building in 1972, and what few he did, Eales ignored. The new building to the rear extends the arms of the H-plan further to the south, but reduces the scale by some fifteen per cent by cutting ceiling heights. Although the roof, parapet and window details are largely duplicated, the stone plinth of the original is replaced by a cheaper brick one, and the whole worked in a brick which fails to match the colour of the older building. Standing on the terrace outside the library, what must have once been a wide view across the Trent valley is now contained by inturned wings which terminate in the incongruous, sculptural forms of two concrete spiral fire escapes.

The first building on the new Highfields campus to be fitted out as a men's hall of residence was the old Lenton Hall, located on the high ground behind the College building and suitably distant from Florence Boot Hall. It was once again Jesse Boot who funded the initial architectural work. In April 1930, he had written from his villa at Cannes to the Honorary Secretary of University College: "It is my intention to bear the entire cost of the present alterations to Lenton Hall to make it suitable for the first 40 students, and then to ascertain what would be the amount involved to extend the accommodation for a further forty . . . I am very anxious to see more hostels around the University, for I attach the greatest possible importance to these as having a great influence on the life of the students, apart from the training they receive at the College."

Boot saw the conversion of Lenton Hall as part of a rolling programme, making use of the contractors already engaged on the other new campus buildings. So it was natural for Morley Horder to be engaged as architect for the new men's hall. Apart from the conversion of the old building, the work involved the addition of, first, five bays (completed by

1931), and then another three (completed in 1932), as a new wing to the north **[34]**. The elevations were unremarkable and although they picked up the rhythm of the windows along the garden front of Lenton Hall, they disrupted the scale, introducing three storeys where there had been just two, and separating the *piano nobile* from the attic storey by the imposition of a string course, a classical reference quite at odds with the Gothick of the older building.

It was not Morley Horder but the Nottingham firm of W B Starr and Hall who made the greatest addition in the early years to Lenton Hall. Taking off from Morley Horder's new wing, they added a new quadrangle, open to the north and stepping down the hill in three flat-roofed blocks. Linked to the garden of Lenton Hall by an axial archway, these blocks are severe and uncompromising, a classicism stripped both of detail and of warmth. Starr and Hall picked up on the lead provided by Morley Horder, repeating the rhythm of his windows, as well as the scale and string course of his façade. The open quadrangle is large, considerably larger than that within the main University College building, and it was probably this, more than anything, which provided Donald McMorran with a starting point for his proposals of 1958, which would have tied the central campus area together so well but were abandoned unrealised, with the exception of the Social Science building off to the west. The new buildings were opened by the Duke of Portland in March 1938, and named after the first principal of the University College at Highfields, Hugh Stewart.

Fig. 34
Extensions to Lenton Hall (now Hugh Stewart Hall) Architect: P Morley Horder 1931/1932

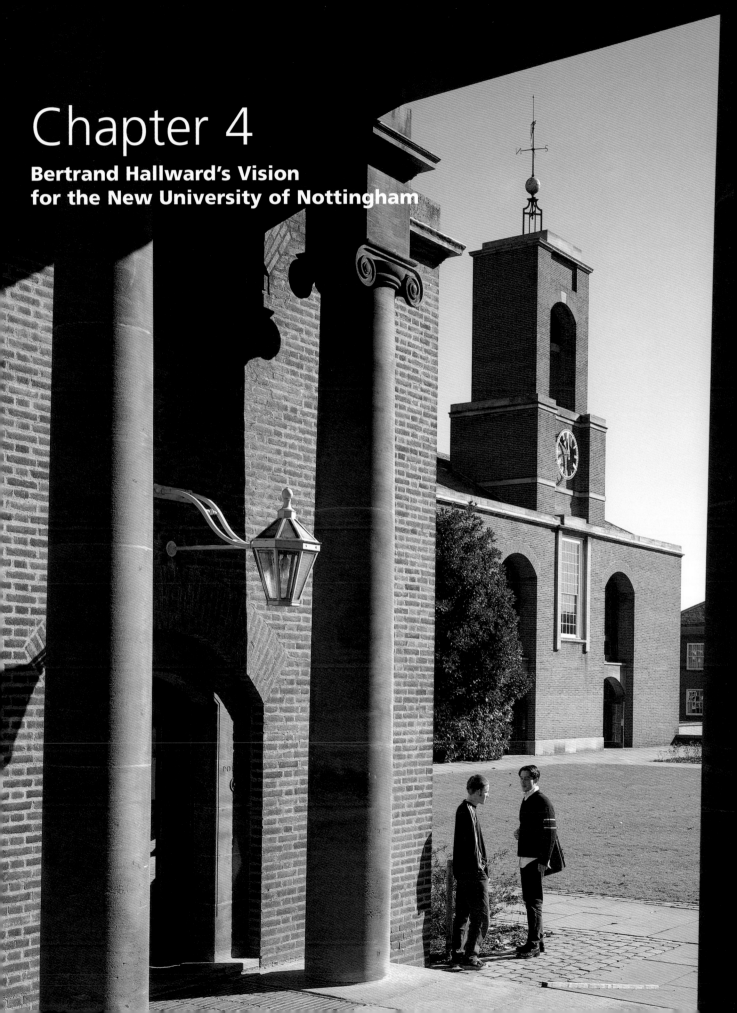

Chapter 4

**Bertrand Hallward's Vision
for the New University of Nottingham**

The Campus Plan

In his annual report to senate of 1950, Vice-Chancellor Bertrand Hallward declared Nottingham to be, "the noblest site of any modern university in this country . . . The splendid conception of the whole plan . . . we owe to Sir Jesse Boot . . . and his brilliant architect, Morley Horder." Horder, although less enthusiastically acclaimed by future generations of architectural critics, had, indeed set the pattern for subsequent development of the 'campus' idea at Nottingham. His prominent siting in 1928 of University College within a mature park at Highfields had its origins in the romantic eighteenth century English gardens of Humphry Repton and Capability Brown, where Palladian country houses had similarly been sited in dramatic contrast to an informal landscape. At Nottingham, in what might be a Reptonian landscape, it proved to be such a potent and enduring image that all subsequent development plans for the campus remained subservient to this central idea.

In 1948 Hallward had approached Sir Percy Thomas with a view to his becoming 'Consultant Architect to the University' and a proposed development plan with associated scale model were ready by December 1949 [35]. By this time, at sixty-six, Thomas was very much a senior figure of the British architectural establishment having already held Presidential office at the Royal Institute of British Architects

Fig. 35

Campus Plan
Architect: Sir Percy Thomas
1949

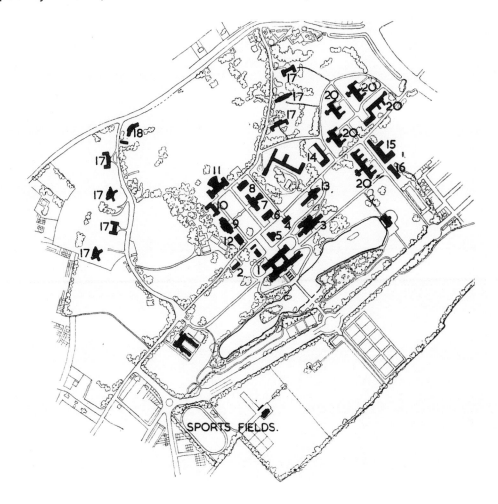

Key

University College
Chapel
Students' Union Building
Spare
Music
Examinations
Lecture Press
University Press
Great Assembly Hall
0 Drama School
1 Library
2 Spare
3 Art School
4 Engineering, Power & Boilers
5 Physical Culture
6 Garages
7 Halls of Residence
8 University Arms Hotel
9 Housing for Staff
0 Science Blocks

twice. His prewar *oeuvre* had subscribed to a mainstream classicism and he seemed a natural successor, therefore, to Horder. Moreover, the classical mode for further campus development had already been reinforced by the appointment of T C Howitt, a prominent Nottingham practitioner, to design a new women's hall of residence, Florence Nightingale Hall, and a new Students' Union building, to be named 'Portland Building' upon completion in October 1956.

Conceived at a time of extreme post-war austerity, Thomas' plan was nothing if not ambitious; its major feature was a grand formal 'square' to the north of the Trent Building. The square was addressed at its northern end by a monumental assembly hall on the same axis as the Trent Building in the best classical Beaux Arts tradition. The plan envisaged humanities departments deployed around this 'piazza' with the sciences relegated to the low-lying eastern end of the campus, whilst halls of residence were to be sited to the north and west separated from the teaching and administrative functions of the university by a green sward or 'down'. The existing west entrance was to be augmented by a formal entrance to the south off a new roundabout on University Boulevard. In spite of a subsequent plan submitted by the landscape architect G A Jellicoe in March 1955, and various interventions by university estates officers since, the principles embodied in the Thomas plan remain evident even to this day.

The first moves to implement the Thomas plan were less than propitious; although a start had been made on Howitt's innovative Nightingale Hall, the same architect's design for a students' union building was postponed. An even worse fate awaited David du R Aberdeen's modernist proposals for a new Botany

and Zoology building in 1950: it was abandoned under pressure from the University Grants Committee in favour of a dreary but more economical design by the university surveyor, J W Popplewell.

Clearly, the ambition of the Thomas plan far exceeded the University's resources; Hallward's frustration was evident in his report to senate in 1950 that building progress had been "arrested and retarded". But there was cause for optimism; recent land acquisition had expanded the University's estate at Highfields to 234 acres (from 88 acres in 1944) and an architectural competition for three halls of residence on the Lenton Fields site had been won by two young architecture lecturers from Tyneside, Turley and Williamson; Nightingale Hall of residence was scheduled to open in January 1951.

In March 1952, Hallward embarked on a three month tour of universities in the United States, an experience which was to strengthen further his commitment to the 'campus' model for a modern university. A similar trip was undertaken by T C Howitt in 1954 which was to consolidate his proposals for the delayed students' union building. It was within this context of an already established plan for the university by Sir Percy Thomas, reinforced by Hallward's recent transatlantic experiences, that G A Jellicoe was engaged to prepare an amended plan for Highfields campus.

G A Jellicoe submitted his proposals to the University in March 1955 by which time he had already established himself as the *doyen* of an emerging profession of landscape architects in postwar Britain [36]. Two years later, the *Architectural Review* referred to Jellicoe's efforts as the Thomas plan "drastically tightened up and re-landscaped", and to a large

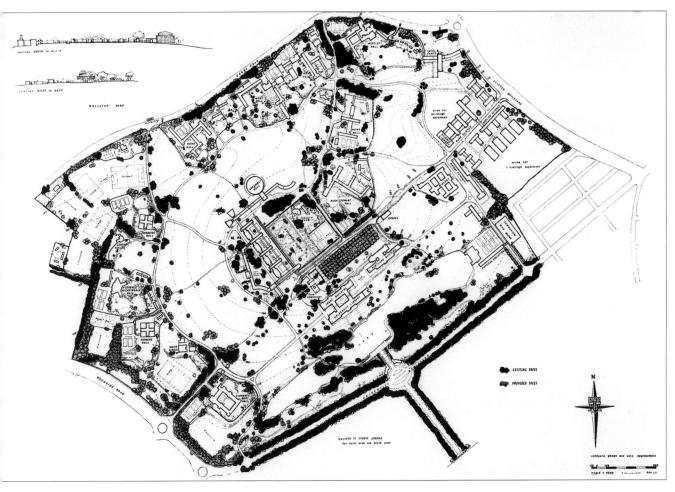

Fig. 36

Campus Plan
Architect: Geoffrey Jellicoe
1955

extent this was so. Indeed, it was Jellicoe's profound understanding of how a carefully fashioned landscape could not only provide an appropriate physical setting for a university, but could also genuinely enhance an undergraduate's existence, that marks his plan as a significant step forward from its predecessor [36].

By today's standards, Jellicoe's associated report is a curiously impassioned document for presentation to a university buildings committee; his proposal for a botanical garden "recalls those at Oxford, Padua and the school of Aristotle; and like the broader landscape, will remind us that whatever may be the conquests of the mind, our bodies must

always 'pass through nature to eternity.'" Jellicoe declared himself also sensitive to climate in preparing his revised plan and was "of the opinion that reasonable and continuous contact with the elements is an essential to hardiness of spirit as well as body". It is not recorded how the University reacted to the unashamedly jingoistic "combat with the English climate . . . has made us self-reliant, . . . determined, . . . as any nation in the world."

Like Thomas, Jellicoe sought to emphasise the Trent Building, the (soon to be completed) Portland Building, and the Vice-Chancellor's lodge as a "peninsula" likened to a mediaeval hill town or monastery, thereby imparting an acceptable academic provenance. Where the plan departed from its predecessor was in its avoidance of Beaux Arts axes; a range of arts faculty buildings enclosed four garden courts and further engaged with a formal landscape devoid of any axial relationship with the Trent Building. Indeed, Jellicoe avoided formal land-scape devices which could have enhanced the Portland Building's potentially overbearing presence to the detriment of the Trent Building's primacy.

Jellicoe's views concerning halls of residence coincided exactly with those of Hallward: "The term, 'residential unit' is dumb, but the use of the word 'hall' instead of 'college' is still all that is needed to describe a university system that is necessarily different in principle from that of the ancient foundations, but nevertheless recognises the virtues of the individual college." His vision for the halls of residence allowed for men's halls to the north responding to the down and for women's halls to the south, much as the plan was subsequently executed. Moreover, Jellicoe articulated an equally clear vision of how such halls could be designed. He envisaged the men's halls "deeply in their grounds" not only engaging with the down, but also looking inward to the busy complex of a landscaped interior. Women's halls were to be "tall", embodying "lightness and grace" in marked contrast to the men's halls which were to be low-rise so as not to interrupt the silhouette of mature trees.

Two other strategic recommendations of the Jellicoe plan were to be fundamental in realising a developed campus: establishing a north entrance and siting the science and engineering buildings "vast and unpredictable as to their future" on level ground at the east of the campus. Jellicoe went on to advise a break with tradition: "The applied sciences need take no note of history or a *genius loci,*" and in typically romantic mode envisaged such a complex as "a restless sea of roofs [with] such lightness and colour and inventiveness of shape as the programme will originate."

Jellicoe's central contribution to the creation of a modern university is indisputable in spite of his all too brief association with Nottingham. But his progressive zeal was not to be reflected in the buildings which appeared at Highfields during the rest of the decade: the work of architects patronised by the university like Donald McMorran, Brian O'Rorke, T C Howitt and his associate, F E Woolley, had been dismissed by the architect and critic, Lionel Brett, as still peddling "the dull axiality of fag-end classicism" long after that great watershed in the history of postwar British architecture, the 1951 Festival of Britain, had established modernism as a mainstream architectural orthodoxy for 'everyman'. Not for another decade after the publication of Jellicoe's plan was the University to demonstrate any profound commitment to the new architecture.

And yet architecture, like all art forms, is subject to massive shifts in taste. A deep and popular dissatisfaction with modernism has produced a reactive backlash of tradition and historicism, encouraged in some quarters as an appropriate architectural stance for the late twentieth century. It is hardly surprising that such a reactionary climate should allow the rehabilitation of this very "fag-end classicism" into an essentially pluralist contemporary architectural culture, a position reinforced, regionally, by Listed Building status being granted to buildings by Donald McMorran and T C Howitt.

T C Howitt and F E Woolley
Portland Building

T C Howitt's completed design for the "proposed union building" was first published in *The Architects' Journal* of 7 July 1949 along with Sir Percy Thomas' master plan for Highfields. The same issue marked the annual conference of the Royal Institute of British Architects which had been held in Nottingham that year and published a preview of forthcoming work from leading local architectural practices. To a new postwar generation of architects committed to the recently imported 'Modern Movement' from Continental Europe it made singularly depressing reading; virtually all those schemes, which included Howitt's students' union building and his half-complete Florence Nightingale Hall, manifested origins in an arguably outworn classical model.

Howitt was typical of the successful inter-war practitioner in provincial England. Born in 1889 (died 1968) in Hucknall, Nottinghamshire, Thomas Cecil Howitt began studying architecture at the Architectural Association in London in 1907, but after a year, he cut short his formal education to set up a London branch for architects Bromley and Watkins, returning to their Nottingham office in 1909. By 1911 he had become an associate member of the Nottingham Society of Architects.

After a highly distinguished army career in the First World War, where he gained the rank of lieutenant-colonel, a DSO and the Croix de Guerre, Howitt returned to Nottingham in 1919 after demobilisation as housing architect to the City Engineer's Department. He was thirty, and his immediate task was to fulfil, for Nottingham, an ambitious 'homes for heroes' national housing programme within the terms of the 1919 Housing and Town Planning Act.

It is certain that within this massive suburban 'garden city' housing programme and by the completion of subsequent civic buildings (most notably Nottingham's Council House of 1929), Howitt did more than any other architect to transmogrify the physical face of Nottingham. His practice was hugely varied and its products generally of great distinction. But it was Howitt's overt traditionalism which was to invite hostile criticism from contemporaneous architectural critics, themselves to a man imbued with the spirit of modernism. In their crusading zeal, they seemed blind to the essential qualities of Howitt's *oeuvre*. His civic and commercial buildings alike command huge presence, most notably the Council House (1929), in the Market Square, Nottingham, the headquarters for Raleigh Cycles (1931), on Radford Boulevard, Nottingham, and the truly monumental Home Brewery (1939), in Daybrook. All of these buildings exhibit a clarity and ingenuity in their *partis* which is also reflected in Howitt's buildings for Highfields. But the subsequent work of his partner and successor, Frederick Woolley, lacks this essential directness, as manifested at Lincoln Hall of residence; here Howitt's axial planning is forsaken for another tradition, that of the English Picturesque.

Cyril Fairey's perspective for Howitt's students' union building depicted a monumental Palladian composition deployed along the contours of a steeply sloping site to the north of the boating lake [37]. Employing the same classical language, and indeed, the same Portland stone cladding as its neighbour, University College, Howitt assembled familiar classical elements in a predictable fashion. A central pavilion with massively-scaled and pedimented portico is flanked by smaller pavilions, set back, and surmounted by balustraded

Fig. 37
Portland Building
Architect: T C Howitt
1957
Perspective drawing: Cyril Fairey
1946

entablatures. The central pavilion has a rusticated ground floor and a recessed attic storey which effectively augments the scale of the central portico and its giant order **[38]**.

The Architects' Journal had described the students' union building as "designed to fit into the University development plan, recently prepared by Sir Percy Thomas," a less than surprising judgement, given the similar architectural predilections of Howitt and Thomas. But where Howitt was to depart from convention was in the organisation of the plan, for the students' union building is not of cellular configuration or *parti* as its elevational treatment might suggest. A massive central staircase, expressed externally by the portico and a bronze, glazed curtain

wall affording splendid views to the south, gives access to generous barrel vaulted concourses which, in turn, connect with the major internal spaces. These are equally generous in their proportions with lofty ceilings and excellent daylighting from tall sash windows.

The Portland Building, as it became known, was conceived from the outset by Bertrand Hallward as "not a students' union building, it is a building built for the whole university of which the students' union is a very important part". This vision was to be reinforced by his subsequent study tour of American universities, but was aimed primarily at arresting a prevailing undergraduate 'nine to five' mentality. According to

Fig. 38
Portland Building
Architect: T C Howitt
1957

Lionel Brett, provincial students spent their lives, "[catching] the 8.30, heavily loaded with books . . . distinguished from other commuters only by tired look and hideous muffler. After a morning of lectures, a queue lunch in a clattering canteen, more lectures . . . they were due back in their digs for high tea . . . On such a day the long journey back . . . for the lecture on Henry Moore . . . hardly seems worthwhile. Much better read by the fire (bob for the meter?) or there's always the landlady's telly." Brett, better known as Viscount Esher, was, presumably, relying on hearsay rather than direct experience of this phenomenon.

Despite the restrictions of its classical dress, the Portland Building, by virtue of its generous spaces and 'open' planning (ironically, pursuits which characterised the opposing 'modernist' camp) went a

long way not only to allay the real concerns expressed by Brett, but also to achieving Hallward's intended lively intercourse amongst the entire university community. He was committed to encouraging a 'long day' policy for students where they could eat, study, debate, visit art exhibitions or buy books at the bookshop all under one roof.

Such lofty ambition met with more enthusiasm than did its architectural expression. *The Architects' Journal* of 9 January 1958, referred to Morley Horder's neighbouring Trent Building as "a formal neo-classic [sic] style . . . [which] . . . gave the university a solid-seeming, essentially worthy background which seems to have once been thought psychologically necessary for a raw young university" **[39]**. However thirty years on from the Trent Building, the

Fig. 39
*Portland Building
Architect: T C Howitt
1957*

same journal expressed some surprise that "Cecil Howitt has continued this eclectic approach by designing a neo-classic [sic] union building . . . stone before and brick behind". Pevsner is similarly unenthusiastic, describing the Portland Building as "[continuing] the classical theme in a much less interesting way [than Horder] with scant regard for the possibilities of the site."

But the critics disregarded a lengthy gestation period for the students' union building imposed by a cautious University Grants Committee in a period of extreme austerity. When formally opened by the Lord Chancellor, Viscount Kilmuir, on 26 October 1956, Howitt's design was already almost a decade old. It was a bold stroke, therefore, to commission the committed modernist, Sir Hugh Casson and his associate, H T Cadbury-Brown, to complete the interior design. Such a shotgun marriage of tradition and modernity potentially could have had disastrous consequences, but the result was highly acclaimed. Recalling his Festival of Britain experience (where he had been coordinating architect), Casson imparted a delicacy to the interiors which compensated for Howitt's rather lumpen exterior. *The Architects' Journal* declared Casson's intervention to be "fresh, colourful and inspiring." Sadly, no trace of this work exists today; nor is the chapel designed for the Portland Building by Lord Mottistone, architect to St. George's Chapel, Windsor, retained in its original form of that of an Oxbridge college **[40]**. The crass re-ordering of

Fig. 40
*Portland Building
Anglican Chapel
Architect: Lord Mottistone
1957*

1994 is now a far cry from what *The Architect and Building News* of 15 August 1957, described as:

. . . Perhaps the most unexpected and dramatic room in the building although it is clear where the original structure ends and how much has been added to give it its present appearance.

The congregation sit in delicately detailed stalls lining either side of the long, narrow room, and these are lit by artificial candle lights in two tiers, one to each member. The 8 volt candle lamps, originally designed for use in the royal houses, are particularly appropriate in this context . . . The emotional effect is heightened by a red curtain hung behind the altar, which glows in the semi-darkness of the space.

Lord Mottistone was better known within the architectural profession as John Seely of Seely and Paget, two young architects who began their careers in the 1920s, fresh from Cambridge. Family connections quickly ensured prestigious clients including Gladys Cooper, J B Priestley, Field-Marshal Lord Montgomery and Stephen Courtauld of the textile dynasty. Seely's other claim to fame is that his 'shack', built at the family seat, Mottistone Manor, was the first modernist building to be acquired by the National Trust.

Howitt's original design allowed for a university theatre to be sited to the north of the Portland Building and connected to it by a generous foyer accessible from the central staircase, accounting for the bleak 'unfinished' outcome of the rear, brick, elevation. Jellicoe had compensated for this in his aborted plan of 1955 by planting a dense linear 'grove' which effectively would have obscured this unfortunate northern aspect.

On completion the Portland Building was not well received by Nottingham's architectural community. To its younger progressive members it seemed unthinkable that a new university's manifest ambition should be served by an architecture of such reactionary mien. Nevertheless, the Portland Building has withstood the test of time particularly well. Despite the loss of Casson's interiors, the assault on Mottistone's chapel, and infelicitous interventions by interior designers since, the essential robustness of Howitt's design remains, responding readily to the changing aspirations of successive generations of undergraduates. After almost half a century therefore, Hallward's prescient vision survives remarkably intact.

Florence Nightingale Hall

Well before the publication of Sir Percy Thomas' campus plan of 1949, the siting of T C Howitt's two major commissions had already been determined. Florence Nightingale Hall, as it became known, was to be sited at Lenton Fields to the west, whilst the students' union building, subsequently the Portland Building, was to be sited alongside University College overlooking the lake to the south. The fundamental planning strategies defining a central area for teaching and administration with peripheral sites to the west and north for student residences therefore had largely been determined even before Thomas' appointment. Thus Nightingale Hall not only generated the campus ethos of halls within the landscape, but was also the first building of any real significance to be completed at the new University of Nottingham.

Howitt had first reached national prominence as a housing architect. The successful interwar public housing programme in Nottingham had been to

Fig. 41
*Florence Nightingale Hall
Architect: T C Howitt
Perspective drawing: Cyril Fairey
1949*

his designs and his skilful handling of domestic scale was to characterise not only his halls of residence but also designs for staff houses associated with them. Freed from the perceived need to create a monument, Howitt produced at Florence Nightingale, even at a time of extreme postwar austerity, a building of appropriate identity and scale which has stood the test of time very well **[41]**.

Fig. 42
*Florence Nightingale Hall
Architect: T C Howitt
1956*

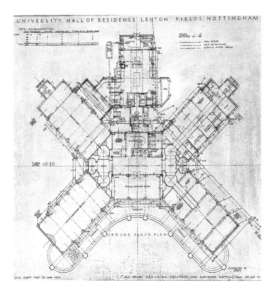

The key to Nightingale Hall's success lies in its clear *parti*; the plan is a double Y evoking the grand pre-war 'butterfly' country house plans adopted by some of Howitt's contemporaries **[42]**. This plan form not only allows for short corridors, notably generous in width at Nightingale, but also for the communal spaces with dual aspect to be accommodated within 'peninsulas' of the Y form. Moreover, the entrance is marked naturally within the Y giving access to an ample ground floor 'concourse' which is repeated on the upper study bedroom floors. The plan also makes good use of its setting by carefully relating common rooms and library to the landscape: a sweeping loggia and associated terrace provide an elegant transition between the two. Belying its heavy exterior, Nightingale Hall's interior spaces are light and airy, with glazed partitions allowing light to penetrate deep into the interior. An attic floor incorporating tutors' flats with associated balconies, provides panoramic views of the campus and beyond.

Fig. 43

*Florence Nightingale Hall
Architect: T C Howitt
1956*

Although Pevsner describes Nightingale Hall as "again, neo-Georgian", familiar classical devices are used in such modified form as to be almost unrecognisable. A massive central pavilion of six storeys surmounted by a pyramidal roof with heavily projecting eaves dominates the symmetrical composition; flanking splayed pavilions of one storey less have corresponding hipped roofs with similarly overhanging eaves and deeply recessed attic floors which step back at their gables to give generous balconies over the floor beneath [43]. This latter device produces a distinctive stepped 'zig-gurat' form to the building, which, reinforced by the ponderous rhythms of the deeply recessed fenestration, imparts a fortress-like quality quite at variance with the delicacy of internal detailing, most particularly the carefully fashioned circular lobbies with domed ceilings which, sited at the splayed junctions of the double-Y plan, provide at ground floor an ingenious interface between the concourse and communal spaces.

Despite its obvious merits, particularly in the deployment of the 'concourse' idea as an armature to connect disparate cellular spaces, Florence Nightingale Hall predictably, given the predilections of contemporaneous critics, attracted less than favourable comment from the architectural press; *The Architects' Journal* of 9 January 1958 declared, "Howitt has designed a women's hostel, a five-finger exercise in planning, five stories high, which is surprisingly bulky for an open country site and yet not high enough to be graceful."

But there could be no equivocation regarding the quality of Howitt's staff housing sited back from the driveway to the hall. Their modest scale effectively tempers the Hall's formality and the 'echelon' siting of the two blocks of semi-detached houses provides a satisfactory prelude to the main building [44].

At a paper delivered to delegates attending the 1949 annual conference of the Royal Institute of British Architects in Nottingham, T C Howitt articulated his

Fig. 44
Staff Housing, Nightingale Close
Architect: T C Howitt
1956

views on housing design, some of which could equally well have been applied to other building types. He urged his architect audience to "rely on the general mass for effect and skyline" whilst employing "really good overhanging eaves." Both are clearly evident in the hall and associated housing. To avoid "semi-detached houses ... [creating] ... a monotonous appearance" Howitt paired a generous family dwelling with a modest tutor's house thereby avoiding a potentially unfortunate elevational 'duality'. Bedroom windows at first floor were recessed above a string course deeply overshadowed by pronounced projecting eaves and bay windows at ground level were deployed for further informal, picturesque effect.

In his deep concern for traditional forms, materials and detailing, Howitt was effectively to set the pattern for subsequent student halls of residence at Highfields: architects of similarly conservative mien were to reinterpret a familiar English collegiate model in a variety of ways to give Nottingham's campus its unique ambience.

Lincoln Hall

The spate of building at Highfields in the late 1950s and early 1960s to create new halls of residence did much to realise Bertrand Hallward's vision for the campus. Architects like McMorran and Whitby, F E Woolley (of Cecil Howitt and Partners) and Brian O'Rorke were favoured by Hallward and Sir Percy Thomas alike for their perceived conservatism, but because of their vastly differing backgrounds, architectural vocabularies and, indeed, skills, the built outcomes varied hugely.

Considering the plethora of precedents for 'collegiate' architecture, Woolley's efforts at Lincoln Hall seem curiously ill-resolved in their stylistic confusion, and, moreover, make little attempt to realise the potential of a westward-sloping site. Indeed, the confusion extends to the landscape, where Arts and Crafts footbridges are juxtaposed with brickwork planting boxes, planned in *echelon* and with stepped section, in a manner more redolent of the Festival of Britain. The plan is similarly eclectic where pavilions of disparate architectural provenance are arranged informally, loosely to enclose a series of 'quadrangles' as the site falls to the west, evoking in the process, the traditional 'ad-hoc' development of Oxbridge colleges. The dining hall, with three hugely-scaled pedimented sash windows facing west over a circular lawn, occupies a commanding position on the east of the site, but access to a flat-roofed anteroom is via a Dutch-gabled entrance which sits unhappily between the massive scale of the dining hall elevation and the single storey junior common room, itself embellished with an oversized timber balustraded parapet and weather-boarded 'pilasters' **[45]**. The effect brings to mind a pastiche of North American campus architecture with which Hallward and Howitt were familiar following their respective visits, in 1952 and 1954, to the United States.

Internally, the dining hall maintains this curious stylistic amalgam, where giant sash windows and corbelled cornice of decidedly classical provenance are juxta-posed with a 'modernist' ceiling with pyramidal coffers. The presence of a kitchen to the east is 'camouflaged' by inserting mirror glass into the lower sashes of the hall's eastern fenestration, hardly a satisfactory solution to reconcile a major volume with its ancillary service areas.

A three-storey 'gatehouse' with pyramidal roof and lantern (recalling Sir John Soane) marks the entrance to the site. Square on plan, with basement and central stair, it accommodates a porter's lodge and associated flats. Externally, weatherboarded quoins form crude, Soanesque 'pilasters' suggesting a giant order, whilst a Palladian staircase to a baroque split-pedimented entrance completes the eclectic mix **[46]**.

Fig. 45
Lincoln Hall dining hall
Architect: F E Woolley
(Cecil Howitt and Partners)
1962

Linear three-storey blocks to the west suggest a lower 'quadrangle' terminated by a temple-like library with Etruscan portico and internal gallery. The library sits unhappily on a pronounced change of level in the site, and the expectation of a free-standing pavilion is hugely compromised by a most infelicitous collision with the adjacent study bedroom block. The double height space is lit by full height sash windows which unfortunately expose the rear of the balcony floor slab. Such contradictions between an internal organisation and its external expression remain difficult to reconcile. For the classicist there is a lack of rigour to the *parti* where any pursuit of Beaux Arts order has been jeopardized by a fey picturesque assembly of disparate forms and motifs; for the modernist, the profound conflict between configuration of internal space and how this is misread externally through elevations, is equally unacceptable **[47]**.

And when completed in 1962, such concerns, particularly those articulated by the modernist camp, seemed even more acute, a position soon reinforced by the publication of progressive designs for the new post-Robbins universities. At a time when British Modernism really had come of age, Woolley's fanciful cocktail at Lincoln Hall seemed a curious anachronism, a throwback to prewar isolationism when a conservative British architectural profession had remained deeply sceptical of progressive movements in Continental Europe.

But within a decade of Lincoln Hall's completion, a reaction to some of modernism's excesses (particularly as manifested in high-rise public housing) was being actively orchestrated by pundit and public alike. One of the many reactionary outcomes was so-called 'post-modernism', a stylistic free-for-all, where architects felt free to quarry the whole of architectural history for their assorted architectural vocabulary. Not surprisingly, given the capriciousness of architectural taste, Lincoln Hall, with its concern for picturesque composition, an application of diverse architectural motifs, and a crafting of permanent traditional building materials, has enjoyed something of a renaissance, in retrospect obscuring to some extent, its profound architectural flaws.

Fig. 47
Lincoln Hall library
Architect: F E Woolley
(Cecil Howitt and Partners)
1962

McMorran and Whitby

Of all the architects brought in to realise Bertrand Hallward and Sir Percy Thomas' vision of the campus, the most interesting and undoubtedly the best were the firm of McMorran and Whitby. Confirmation of this lies not only in the fact that their design for Cripps Hall is the one postwar Listed Building on campus, but that this design was included in the first listing of postwar buildings made by the Department of the Environment. In comparison with Cripps Hall, it is surprising, therefore, that their two other contributions to the campus, the Social Sciences (now Education) Building and Lenton Hall, are really so bland.

Although George Whitby had joined Donald McMorran in partnership in 1958, just a year or so after work began on Cripps Hall, it is McMorran's name which is most usually linked, at least in the architectural press, with this and the other buildings. Nevertheless, the firm of McMorran and Whitby became associated with an architecture which, by its very conservatism, secured them a reputation. McMorran died in 1965 and Whitby eight years later. On this latter occasion the architect John Brandon Jones wrote to *The Times*:

McMorran and Whitby were among leaders of the small band of architects who have demonstrated the possibility of applying classical principles in the design of large, modern buildings. Over and over again they were able to show that the traditional formulae were capable of infinite variety and also that, for many purposes, traditional materials and craftsmanship could still compete successfully with system building from the economic as well as the aesthetic point of view. Their buildings have qualities of austere elegance and dignity that will be very hard to match, and their work will remain a challenge and an inspiration to many younger architects, disillusioned by mass production and by the aridity of so much contemporary design.

McMorran was very much an establishment figure. He had worked for Vincent Harris, architect of the Manchester Central Reference Library, had become an Associate of the Royal Academy in 1955, Master of the Art Workers Guild in 1956, and between 1955 and 1958 had chaired the National Joint Consultative Committee for the RIBA. He had, as his obituary in *The Times* noted, "became a well-known figure in the profession, although his sympathies were largely those of an earlier generation." It is surprising, therefore, that, as an assessor for the famous Golden Lane housing competition of 1952, he had selected the progressive scheme of the unknown firm of Chamberlin, Powell and Bon. It served to make their reputation and to establish a new and modernist look to the buildings of the City of London. Nevertheless, *The Times* concluded, "he was in general, however, a vigorous critic of modern architecture and a firm upholder of his own more traditional beliefs."

Cripps Hall

If there is a quality evident in all three of McMorran and Whitby's buildings on campus, it is in their clarity of form and arrangement. As *The Builder* commented in November 1962, on the occasion of McMorran's election as a Royal Academician, "Mr McMorran is out of the Vincent Harris stable . . . and this is shown by his direct logical planning and fine sense of massing." Cripps Hall is structured with an almost rigid axiality, but one which provides order rather than formality. The entrance is understated, more of a window than a gateway, framing the view across the Trent

Fig. 48
Cripps Hall
architect: McMorran and Whitby
1957

valley. The first quadrangle, grassed and open to the south is dominated by the bellcote and clock-tower set above the entrance to the dining hall whose presence is signified by the range of tall windows along the east side of the quadrangle. The bellcote and clock-tower also commands the one dominant and noticeable axis in the plan **[48]**. This runs from the tower, along the south end of the first quadrangle, down some steps, and then along the north side of the second quadrangle, thus linking the two, to disappear through a double archway on the west side of this lower space. Similar axes, once noticed, can be identified in a number of instances, linking door with door, and door with archway, thus providing pathways which the desire-lines of a now more selfish

society tend to ignore. Thus the composition is tuned and balanced, vertical mass playing off against horizontal movement, symmetrical elevations complemented by well-composed, asymmetrical edifices.

Cripps Hall, founded in 1957, is just one of a number of contemporaneous designs in which McMorran tried out similar themes. The first and the largest was the Lammas Green Housing Estate at Sydenham, London, completed by 1957. Here 27 houses and 30 flats were grouped around a small green, quadrangular and open-cornered as at Cripps Hall. The three-storey blocks of flats, built of hand-made Essex bricks with parapet gutters, tall chimneys and sash windows in flush surrounds, further

recall Cripps Hall. McMorran's design for the King's School at Chester, exhibited at the Royal Academy Summer Exhibition in 1958, a year before the drawings for Cripps Hall were hung, show a similar use of axial planning and balanced massing around an open quadrangle. Although twinned archways and tall windows were again a feature, the architecture was of that stripped modernism which alluded to Scandinavia without being outright European. More home-grown was the County Hall at Exeter [49], described by Pevsner as "long ranges of buff brick in a pleasant, slightly bland, but well-detailed semi-Georgian idiom

of 1957-64." This description, if not the actual date, could be written of Cripps Hall. Indeed, the architecture was so similar that photographs of one might well be mistaken as being of the other [50].

The quality which sets Cripps Hall apart from its siblings is as much to do with scale as it is to do with attention to detail, for the compactness of the one is well-balanced by the richness of the other. While not being obviously derivative, McMorran demonstrates a mastery of neo-Georgian design drawn not so much from the eighteenth (or even late-seventeenth) century, but from the

Fig. 51
Cripps Hall entrance
Architect: McMorran and Whitby
1957

beginning of the twentieth: thus he returns to the architecture of his youth. The axiality of the plan is something one would associate with Lutyens - Deanery Gardens at Sonning (1910), for instance. More obvious, if not just for its idiosyncrasy, is the entrance with its Ionic volutes turned against the line of the elevation and set under the deep eaves of the oversailing roof **[51]**. Here McMorran could have been looking at the stable gateway Lutyens built at Nashdom in Buckinghamshire (1910). For the pyramidal roof and central chimney of the warden's house **[52]**, it could have been Lutyens' Gledstone Hall in Yorkshire (1923) which he had in mind. There is also something of Lutyens' castles in the stone vaulted minstrels gallery at one end of the great hall, and something of his Home Counties houses in the panelled, polygonal bay window set low into the wall behind the high table at the other end **[53]**. But the heavy, beamed mahogany roof in between is neither of Lutyens nor successful. Nevertheless, throughout the building, from the architraves of the staircase doors with their rusticated stonework and inset footscrapes, to the oak-faced bookcases and vaulted ceiling of the library **[54]**, the details are good and the architecture sound. It is therefore a shame that the additions of 1968 by Cartwright Woollatt take so little notice of the axial arrangement and so little heed of the detailing.

Lenton Hall

Axiality is the theme behind the arrangement of Lenton Hall, built to the west of Redcourt, by McMorran and Whitby in 1965. Set on sloping land, like Lincoln Hall opposite, Lenton Hall does not step down the hillside as might be expected - and, indeed, as Lincoln Hall does - but rather straddles the contours, the buildings arranged in a series of

Fig. 53
Cripps Hall dining hall
Architect: McMorran and Whitby
1957

Fig. 54
Cripps Hall library
Architect: McMorran and Whitby
1957

parallel lines along the hillside **[55]**. The result is that the contained space of the quadrangle, a plateau of cut-and-filled earth, is not immediately appreciated on entering. This is because the middle range on the east side is set some metres uphill, a grassy bank and a large chestnut tree encroaching upon the space; and because the middle range on the west side is similarly set back but also dropped down a whole storey onto a lower terrace. Thus the sense of enclosure which these buildings should have provided is somewhat dissipated. It is only when viewed from the dining hall at the far, north end, that the geometry of the quadrangle becomes noticeable. For now the space works particularly well, the flanking blocks stepping out

and stepping in again to frame, beyond the porter's lodge which is set like a gunsight at the end of a barrel, a distant view across the down.

What Lenton Hall lacks most of all is a proper entrance. A number of side entrances, each on significant yet secondary cross-axes allow access from Redcourt (its library and nursery window bay terminating one such axis) and the upper lawns on one side, and from Lenton Hurst and the lower terraces on the other. But along the main axis, which stretches between the porter's lodge and the dining hall, there is no point of entry. The porter's lodge, based upon the younger William Wilkins' Gower Street gate lodges at University College,

Fig. 56
Lenton Hall porter's lodge
Architect: McMorran and Whitby
1965

London, appears more like a summer-house than a security point [56]. It guards what should be the entrance, had the plateau of the central space been allowed to spread out towards the road. But in the event this edge of the quadrangle is closed off by an iron fence and entry is gained only by a slippery side-step around its end.

In addition to the primary (north/south) and secondary (east/west) axis which set up the open spaces between the buildings, a series of tertiary, east/west axes serve to connect corresponding entrances to hallways and staircases in the dormitory and dining blocks. Furthermore, a fourth series of axes, now running north/south, follow the ridge lines of the parallel blocks, their presence made noticeable by the white, boarded pediments which crown each gable elevation. These pediments, like triangular topsails in a crowded harbour, provide a sense of order amongst the ranged rooftops **[57]**. McMorran had used such a feature to similar effect in an earlier, hillside scheme: the 27 houses on the Lammas Green Estate at Sydenham.

Compared with Cripps Hall, where some £400,000 of private funding allowed for a richer architecture, Lenton Hall appears, as has been noted, rather bland. This is as much due to the choice of pale bricks and white paintwork, as it is to the lack of articulation in the wall surfaces and shallow relieving arches

over many of the windows. Even in the dining hall, where a sense of scale could have made a grand space, the use of a low, timber-trussed roof, half-panelled walls and boarded recesses, reduces the image from the collegiate to the comprehensive. In short, the building lacks vigour.

Social Sciences Building

McMorran and Whitby's Social Sciences Building was completed in 1961. Located behind the Trent Building between Highfield House and The Orchard, (a house designed in 1904 by W Dymock Pratt for Alfred Thomas

Fig. 57

Lenton Hall
Architect: McMorran and Whitby
1965

Richards, manager of the Imperial Laundry on Radford Boulevard, and now serving as the School of Politics **[58]**,) the Social Sciences Building was to form the west side of McMorran's central campus plan of 1958 **[59]**. This accounts for its size, shape and asymmetry, for it was to be part of a larger complex of grand buildings of which the Trent and

Portland Buildings were to form the southern edge. McMorran's plan would have worked well, for it would have taken the scale of the two older buildings up the downs, through the medium of a grand piazza of almost urban proportions, composed of L- and T-shaped buildings housing the arts faculty. And beyond this, closing off one corner, was to be the Social Sciences Building, its long arms reaching out into the landscape. As *The Builder* observed: "Though standing by itself, the siting and form of this building have been carefully studied so as to contribute to the total effect." But the plan was dropped and the site reclaimed by the "cowsheds", or the "Cherry Tree Buildings" as they are more prettily known, leaving the Trent and Portland Buildings hanging, unrelated, on the edge of the escarpment.

The peculiar, extended U-plan of McMorran and Whitby's Social Sciences Building now sits within a congested landscape, caught between the delivery

Fig. 60

Social Sciences Building and the
Department and Institute
of Education
Royal Academy drawing
of preliminary design
Architect: McMorran and Whitby
1958

bay of the Hallward Library and the proposed Millennium Garden. The building is best described as a long, axial corridor with two wings projecting to the rear and a distinct but attached block free standing to the front **[60]**, **[61]**. This last is the lecture theatre which is placed to

one side of the north entrance lobby and courtyard. It is a single storey building which, due to the rising site, is set, like the north entrance, at second floor level. Here the scale is small and compact. The lower end of the main building, where the south entrance is

Fig. 61

Social Sciences Building
Architect: McMorran and Whitby
1961

located, rises to three storeys and more, an octagonal cupola set above the entrance, and assumes a grander appearance. Thus the building has two aspects, much as the allocation of accommodation would suggest: the Department and Institute of Education were at the upper, north end, while the Departments of Geography, Economics, and Industrial Economics were located at the lower end, identified by the cupola. Psychology and Social Science held the rather uncomfortable ground in the middle.

Although the building hosted a variety of departments and was set upon a sloping site, McMorran and Whitby gave it a visual coherence while at the same time providing the elevations with some individuality. Tall windows, as at the south end, identified lecture rooms, and an arcade the entrance. Shallow arches, a feature already used at Cripps Hall and to be repeated at Lenton Hall, articulated the ground floor, until it was run to earth, and then expressed the screen wall which closed off the court between the Education lecture theatre and the north entrance. Paired arches, as at Cripps Hall and, contemporaneously, at the King's School at Chester, served the north entrance and the series of axial openings which terminated in the screen of the adjacent court. And behind the arcade of the south entrance another paired archway provided the only way in **[62]**.

Internally, there is a sense of heaviness which the lightness of the elevations does not suggest. Long, barrel-vaulted corridors run off where a flat ceiling would be expected and, elsewhere, passageways pass through walls so thick they might be mediaeval. *The Builder,* however, explained:

The structure of this building is unusual among recent university buildings of its kind. No reinforced concrete frame has been used and the floors and the loads they support are carried by the external brick walls and carefully selected internal ones. The stresses in the walls have been calculated in the same manner as those in a reinforced concrete column.

The intention was to exact considerable economies from the structure and thus provide a far higher quality of finish, and a much faster building programme, than was usually obtainable in such buildings.

The whole of the internal joinery is solid hardwood. The roof is covered in Westmorland slate and lead, and the highest quality Leicestershire bricks are used, with Portland Stone, for facings. As a result, it is expected that the building will cost little to maintain. This structural method has the advantage of speeding the build.

The building work was, indeed, fast. The whole of the Social Science section was handed over within fourteen months, and Education followed four months later. But despite its elegant detailing - the hidden gutters are worthy of study - and careful and solid workmanship apparent to anyone using the building, it remains rather forlorn. This is, perhaps, because it is a large building which seems to step back defensively from its site, and where it does encompass the landscape, as in the quadrangle to the rear or in the smaller court by the north entrance, it does nothing with it. Near the south entrance there is a bronze statue of D H Lawrence, trouser legs rolled up and clutching a delicate, purple flower: this is the only connection this building makes with the land around it.

Brian O'Rorke
Derby Hall

Never less than acerbic, Nikolaus Pevsner, writing in the Nottinghamshire edition of his *Buildings of England* series, dismissed "the six halls built in 1954-60 by a team of architects under Sir Percy Thomas [as] built on the collegiate plan in 'Wrenaissance' style with formal gardens and quadrangles totally at odds with this part of the park. What a chance was missed to exploit the informal possibilities of modern architecture." Despite its distinguished origins, the epithet 'Wrenaissance' was one of derogation, suggesting not only an outdated architecture when completed in 1963, but also one reliant upon excessively overworked, Mannerist detail, generally English Baroque.

Whilst this criticism may fairly be applied to Lincoln Hall in its meretricious application of such detail, the same cannot be said of its westerly neighbour, Derby Hall, where 'Wrenaissance' gives way to spare, minimalist detailing verging on the ascetic. Moreover, where Lincoln Hall pursues the 'picturesque' with an informal grouping of buildings, Derby Hall employs a rigorous axiality where formal relationships between the various parts of the building adhere to well-tried Beaux Arts principles.

For the design of Derby Hall, Sir Percy Thomas appointed the New Zealander, Brian O'Rorke. O'Rorke received his architectural education at the Architectural Association, London, after the First World War but well before that institution had

Figs. 63
Derby Hall
Architect: Brian O'Rorke
Perspective drawings
1960

Fig. 64
*Derby Hall
Architect: Brian O'Rorke
1963*

embraced any notions of Continental modernism. His architectural background was therefore firmly classical, although he did produce in the inter-war years a series of houses in the Arts and Crafts idiom.

Derby Hall is not only dominated by notions of symmetry and axiality but also by a carefully contrived architectural promenade **[63]**. Two short three-storey blocks of study bedrooms provide a forecourt or prelude to the entrance, a classical arched *propylaeum* with pitched copper roof accommodating the porter's lodge and bicycle sheds. The route then drops into the main quadrangle formed from two three-storey study bedroom blocks; that to the south is based on the Oxbridge 'sets' with associated staircases, whilst the U-shaped block to the north is arranged around corridor access.

The axial route then passes through a hugely scaled portico giving access to an entrance hall with formal staircase to the library at first floor. Square on plan, the library is lit by a slender lantern on the main axis and clearly identified from the quadrangle and entrance route. The dining hall with its dais and top table as axial stop, provides a most satisfactory climax to this carefully articulated architectural promenade.

The planning of ancillary accommodation and the linkages effected between study bedroom blocks are similarly well contrived so that Derby Hall is perceived as a whole where disparate elements contribute to a rigorous and comprehensible entity. The kitchen and service areas are sited to the north, cleverly concealed from Beeston Lane by screen walls with blind arcading, a device evoking the use of stable blocks to complete the architectural composition of eighteenth century English country houses. Loggias not only provide a covered route between

residential blocks and central facilities, but extend the flattened arch *motif* throughout the composition. A further two-storey range of tutors' flats and guest rooms completes the composition to the northwest balanced by a modest warden's house with views over the down to the southwest.

O'Rorke's command of detailing and materials is equally rigorous. Using a limited palette of materials applied to an equally spare range of architectural *motifs,* Derby Hall presents a minimalist architectural expression totally appropriate to the building's powerful *parti* **[64]**. Devices like the recessed blind arcading at ground floor level and parapets with concealed gutters impart a satisfying scale to the study bedroom blocks, further reinforced by shallow reveals to window openings so that the intervention of the fenestration pattern upon the elevations is minimal. The only disruption is the mannered brick "shutters" to the bathroom windows. Alongside such bland elevational treatment, idiosyncratic entrances to the study bedroom blocks make for welcome relief and in their careful assembly of abstract forms, evoke the work of Sir John Soane: projecting brickwork 'pilasters' support masonry spheres with projecting canopies and semi-circular arches with blind reveals overhead **[65]**.

In retrospect, the true significance of Derby Hall lies in its appeal to traditionalists and progressives alike. Traditionalists are drawn by overt historicist references to a collegiate typology and to hints of 'Soanesque' stripped classical detail, whilst those of modernist tendencies are drawn to the rational planning and minimalist detail. Although finished within months of its eclectic neighbour, Lincoln Hall, Derby Hall presents a much more durable face of tradition.

Fig. 65
Derby Hall
Architect: Brian O'Rorke
1963

Chapter 5
Modern Architecture for Highfields and Sutton Bonington

The Shift to Modernism

The appointment of Sir Percy Edward Thomas (1883-1969) in 1948 as "consultant architect to the university" seemed a less than propitious start for modern architecture at Highfields. Thomas had come fresh from his prewar proposals for the new Penglais campus at University College, Aberystwyth, and indeed, his substantial commissions for University College of South Wales and Monmouthshire at Cardiff. All were to exhibit that familiar flat, ponderous classicism which from many hands was to blight university building in Britain prior to the watershed of the 1963 Robbins Report.

Within such a context, then, David du R Aberdeen's appointment in 1949 to design a new building for the Departments of Botany and Zoology came as a welcome surprise [66]. Aberdeen was a committed modernist and was to gain a national reputation for his brilliant competition-winning entry for the Trades Union Congress headquarters building in Great Russell Street, London (1957). Like that of the TUC building, Aberdeen's plan for Botany and Zoology was notably clear; a central core of shared lecture theatres was linked to ranges of teaching and laboratory spaces to north and south all accom-

Fig. 66

Departments of Botany and Zoology unbuilt project architect: David du R Aberdeen 1949

UPPER GROUND FLOOR

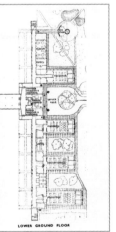

LOWER GROUND FLOOR

modated within copper-clad reinforced concrete shell domes. Further spurs of research laboratories ran at right angles to the main north-south concourse, giving more than a hint of a well-established Bauhaus 'finger planning' strategy.

Had Aberdeen's design been built, it would have established an uncompromising modernism not only at Highfields but regionally. *The Architects' Journal* of 7 July 1949 devoted no less than three pages to the project, such was its perceived national importance, but by 1958 the same journal had tempered its enthusiasm somewhat, declaring the scheme to be a "rather aggressively modern shell-domed project." Ironically, its projected completion in summer 1951 would have coincided exactly with the Festival of Britain, an event which not only gave modernism official approval but invested such progressive architecture with populist appeal.

The University was to wait another decade before demonstrating a firm commitment to modernism. Basil Spence (ironically, the architect who arguably had made the greatest single contribution to the Festival of Britain with his designs for the 'Transport' and 'Sea and Ships' pavilions) was engaged formally in 1958, although initial overtures from the University had been made following publication of the Jellicoe plan, to prepare an overall development plan for science and engineering buildings on a level site at the east of the campus. As early as 1948 negotiations had begun to acquire the Clifton Boulevard site from the City ultimately for science and engineering buildings, but with a view to leasing, in the short term what *The Architects' Journal* referred to as "a typical MOW brick-built slum of hutments sprawling in wasteland".

Spence gained popular and national acclaim following his winning entry for the Coventry Cathedral architectural competition in 1950 (completed in 1962) but had previously enjoyed a brilliant career both as student in the inter-war years and as young practitioner, being appointed by Sir Edwin Lutyens to assist in designing the Viceroy's House at New Delhi. In the postwar years his practice soon developed an impressive portfolio of university buildings, most notably his unashamedly eclectic scheme for Sussex University and when complete, his buildings at Nottingham were to exhibit similarly eclectic tendencies. Just as the traditionalists appointed by Sir Percy Thomas at Highfields were to trawl the whole gamut of classical precedent for their architectural vocabulary, so Spence looked to a surprisingly diverse range of modernist architectural 'icons' as models for his eclectic palette. References to Le Corbusier, Mies van der Rohe, less emphatically to Paul Rudolph and even to the Scandinavian school, abound in the buildings for Science City as designed by Spence and his partner and successor, Andrew Renton. By engaging in such pluralist architecture within a range of traditional materials, Spence was not only able to avoid the repetitiveness which so bedevilled mainstream modernism in the eyes of a sceptical public, but also gained acceptance amongst a university community at Nottingham so far firmly wedded to tradition.

In its final form, Spence's master plan for the science and engineering buildings was published in a 'Preview' edition of the *Architectural Review* for January 1960. Like his plan for science buildings at the University of Exeter, and, indeed, Gollins, Melvin and Ward's scheme for Sheffield University, all published in the same issue, the outcome followed a familiar pattern of

Fig. 67
Master Plan for Science and Engineering
Architect: Basil Spence 1959

rectilinear, flat-roofed blocks enclosing an hierarchical arrangement of open spaces and courtyards ranging from public to semi-private **[67]**. Spence had also deployed a tower block with east-west aspect as a vertical element to complete the abstract three-dimensional composition just as he had done at Exeter and, indeed, as had appeared in Gollins' scheme for Sheffield. The plan reflected a modernist orthodoxy for urban architecture which could well be applied to universities or new town 'precincts' alike and which had been clearly articulated in Le Corbusier's well-publicised but unbuilt project for the town centre of Saint Dié, in northern France, in 1945.

Nevertheless, the University still remained ambivalent in its commitment to the new architecture, for as Spence was preparing his proposals for Science City, the arch-conservative, Donald McMorran, had already been commissioned to prepare *his* plan for the central area of the campus to the north of the Trent and Portland buildings. Not surprisingly, in its crafted 'collegiate' architecture, this project represented the antithesis of Spence's progressive aspirations, a situation reflecting exactly the prevailing "two cultures" as articulated contemporaneously by the Cambridge don C P Snow **[68]**.

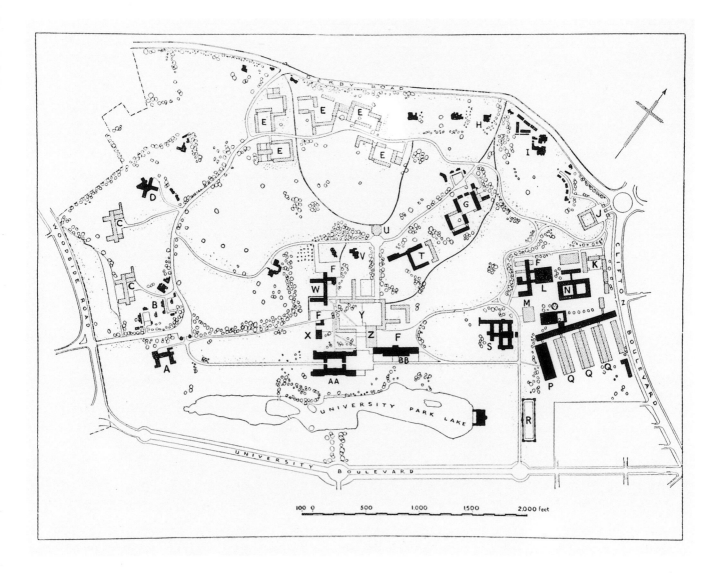

Fig. 68

*Campus Plan representing the
"two cultures"
Central Area Architect:
McMorran and Whitby
Science and Engineering
Architect:
Basil Spence*

KEY TO PLAN

AA	Trent Building
BB	Portland Building
A	Florence Boot Hall (Women)
B	Staff Houses and Music School
C	Proposed Halls for Women
D	Florence Nightingale Hall (Women)
E	Proposed Hall for Men
F	Car Park
G	Cripps Hall (Men)
H	Paton Congregational College
I	Wortley Hall (Men)
J	Proposed Main Entrance
K	Proposed Pharmacy Building
L	Physics Building

M	Proposed Science Library
N	Chemistry Building
O	Applied Science First Year Teaching Building
P	Mining and Fluids Laboratory
Q	Proposed Applied Science Laboratories
R	Swimming Pool
S	Biology Building
T	Hugh Stewart Hall (Men)
U	Proposed University Chapel
V	University Club
W	Social Sciences & Education Building
X	Vice-Chancellor's House
Y	Proposed Central Court
Z	Proposed Great Hall & Theatre

But Spence's first commission for the University was not even destined for the Highfields campus. The Midland Agricultural College, designed by the Leicester architects, Pick Everard, in 1915, for a site at Sutton Bonington **[69]**, had been transferred to University College in 1947 and was renamed the School of Agriculture. It was the University's Agricultural Science building at the Sutton Bonington campus which was to provide Spence with his initial modernist essay at Nottingham. The result, first published in the January 1957 issue of *Architectural Review* **[70]** was an assured three-storey, spine corridor slab block, with the obligatory flat roof and curtain walling (but utilising pre-cast concrete panels when built **[71]**), which demonstrated that a progressive architecture could well serve the requirements of university science departments of equal ambition. Further in Spence's favour was a site well removed from an established classicism at Highfields.

By the beginning of the 1960s, Sir Percy Thomas had retired as master planner for the university campus and in 1962 the South African-born, Sir William Graham Holford, was appointed in his place. Like his predecessor, and indeed, like Spence, Holford had been President of the Royal Institute of British Architects, and was to emerge very much as an establishment

Fig. 70
Agricultural Science Building
Sutton Bonington
Preliminary Design
Architect: Basil Spence 1956

Fig. 71
Agricultural Science Building
Sutton Bonington
Architect: Basil Spence 1958

figure, gaining a peerage in 1965. In 1961 Holford had been asked to prepare a report on the use of the Trent Building as a new university library, a proposal which had been aired initially in the 1955 Jellicoe plan for Highfields. Soon after his appointment, Holford became involved in proposals for a sports centre, a joint venture with the City. This was rejected ultimately in 1964 by the City's Baths and Parks Committee, so Holford's collaborative initiative came to nought. Beside the ambition of the Thomas plan **[72]** and more particularly the Jellicoe plan which succeeded it in 1955 **[73]**, the evidence of Holford's incumbency as campus planner seems slight. In view of his dismissal of the University, in conversation with Professor Brian Tate, as a "fruit cocktail of a campus", this is hardly surprising.

But the spate of building at Nottingham during the 1960s merely reflected a national picture of post-Robbins euphoria within the university sector. Not surprisingly, this wave of optimism was to be identified firmly with so-called 'modernism' which very rapidly displaced traditional attitudes as an orthodoxy for university building. "[Freshmen] will probably be the first generation of students whose academic environment is neither Gothic, Classic [sic] nor Revivalistic but dominantly modern", trumpeted the *Architectural Review* in October 1963, and added, "the current wave of building and rebuilding in British universities, the founding of new ones and the raising of other institutions to university status, have produced an unprecedented situation in British university architecture, a situation which

Fig. 72
Campus Plan
Architect: Sir Percy Thomas
1949

Fig. 73
*Campus Plan
Architect: Geoffrey Jellicoe,
1955.
Jellicoe's vision of halls of
residence set in the landscape*

favours modern architecture". Further-more, such building activity gave a tremendous boost to a rapidly changing architectural profession in Britain following the post-war years of austerity, as newly-established practices gained national reputations on the back of university commissions. Moreover, many fledgling architects who cut their teeth at architects' offices engaged in university work during the 1960s were to achieve national and international reputations by the 1990s. It is more than coincidental that Sir Michael Hopkins, as a young assistant, had worked on Nottingham's applied science buildings in Spence's London office.

But despite such activity, the late 1950s and 1960s at Highfields were to be characterised also by projects which never saw the light of day. Even by 1955, for example, the siting of a purpose-designed university chapel was again revived in Jellicoe's plan: a prominent elevated location terminating a formal 'grove' behind the Portland Building was mooted. In 1963 the question of a university chapel raised its head again, precipitated by a £100,000 benefaction towards the project. A modest archi-tectural competition was initiated but the outcome was an even more modest reordering of surplus space in the basement of the Portland Building, to a striking design based upon a traditional Oxbridge chapel, by Lord Mottistone.

In 1962 Williamson, Faulkner Brown and Partners submitted plans for a university theatre and an assembly hall to be sited behind the Portland Building more or less according to the McMorran plan of 1958 for the campus central area. But by 1963 the University Grants Committee had rejected the scheme on cost grounds by which time, incidentally, Holford had been appointed as campus master planner and proposals for a formal central 'square' were to be amended yet

Fig. 74
University Theatre
unbuilt project
Architect: Williamson
Faulkner Brown and Partners
1962

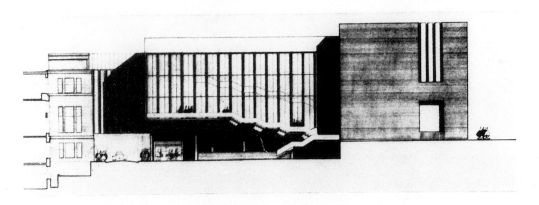

again. Nevertheless, the architects felt sufficient confidence in the theatre's ultimate materialisation to publish the scheme in the January 1965 'Preview' issue of the *Architectural Review* [74]. The plan was symmetrically disposed about the axis of the Portland Building and would have entailed the long overdue demolition of Cherry Tree Buildings. A generous foyer was linked to social spaces within the Portland Building and wrapped around the egg-like 750-seat auditorium. Grand external staircases echoed those internally as part of an inventive architectural promenade. A 500-seat cinema was sited in the basement. However the fixed end-stage configuration did nothing to reflect prevailing notions of flexibility in theatre design and, had it been built in this form, the building would have imposed severe restrictions on any theatrical producer with such aspirations. The design in its limited ambition contrasted sharply with Peter Moro's flexible experimental drama studio for Hull University published simultaneously. In the event the theatre was reduced to a modest adaptation of part of the old engineering building, dressing rooms being added in 1968 for a theatre 'workshop'. Similarly, provision for sporting activity for undergraduates

had featured prominently in both the Thomas and Jellicoe plans for the university, yet Holford's ambition to establish a joint Sports Centre with the city was thwarted.

In 1961 Sir William Holford had also reactivated the whole question of a new university library and prepared a report on the feasibility of reordering the Trent Building for this purpose, a proposal initiated by Jellicoe in 1955. One radical aspect of Holford's plan was to roof over the central quadrangle of the Trent Building creating a vast atrium foyer space. Funding for this scheme was not forthcoming but in 1963 Williamson, Faulkner Brown and Partners were commissioned to prepare a scheme for a new library building on a site to the north of the Portland Building. Further problems surrounding University Grants Committee funding delayed completion of the project until August 1972. Although rightly acclaimed by the contemporaneous architectural press, the new library, on account of its revised location on Library Road, scotched forever any notion of creating a university central square as envisaged in all university master plans since that of Sir Percy Thomas in 1948.

Halls of Residence

The latter half of the decade also witnessed architects of modernist persuasion being commissioned to design halls of residence for an ambitious programme of new foundations and extensions to those already well established. Whilst the architectural predilections of the first Vice-Chancellor, Bertrand Hallward, had coincided with those of his master-planner, Sir Percy Thomas, to produce exclusively classical halls of residence, by 1965 Hallward had retired and Thomas had been replaced in 1962 by the less conservative Holford. More specifically, the withdrawal of the Mancunian arch-traditionalist Hubert Worthington from the commission to design Sherwood and Rutland halls of residence facilitated the appointment of the modernist, J Fletcher Watson, for this task. Finally, it seemed that the dead hand of classical tradition at Highfields was to be displaced by an architecture more attuned to the spirit of the age, but Watson was not from that *avant-garde* coterie of architects favoured by the emerging, new universities. The outcome at Sherwood and Rutland, in 1965, was, therefore, a peculiarly eclectic, but quintessentially English interpretation of the new architecture. Both halls were designed with a view to reinterpreting the traditional collegiate quadrangle using contemporary forms and materials. Rutland is by far the more successful in this pursuit, employing an effective recessed cloister [75], whilst Sherwood's two storey quadrangle loses all pretence at collegiality, resembling more a suburban flat development. Both halls suffer from an excess of the 'picturesque' by the siting of self-conscious weather-boarded pavilions on stilts at key locations in the halls' respective plans. This essentially romantic manifestation of modernism had its origins more in the English picturesque tradition than in any Continental model: it was pejoratively classified as 'peoples' detailing' by the architectural critic, Charles Jencks [76].

Fig. 75

Rutland Hall
Architect: J Fletcher Watson
1965

Fig. 76
Rutland Hall
Architect: J Fletcher Watson
1965

Much less assured was Cartwright, Woollatt and Partners' extension to Hugh Stewart Hall of residence, completed in 1968, and a less than fitting response not only to the original castellated façade of 1792, but also to Starr and Hall's extension of 1938.

Although the competition for a women's hall of residence and site planning for four such halls had been published in May 1950, the winning entry by two young Durham University architecture lecturers, Turley and Williamson, was not to be reactivated until fifteen years later. Sir Percy Thomas had been the assessor and the competition conditions were nothing if not stringent: a central corridor planning strategy for the study bedrooms

was stipulated along with materials which would "mellow with age". Thomas, although lauding the winning entry as "neither too compact nor too sprawling" was damning of other entrants' efforts "which might well be suitable for a hospital". In similar critical vein he stated that, "the elevational treatment [of unsuccessful entries] varies . . . from the traditional collegiate Tudor to the very modern, neither of which in my opinion meets the wishes of your [university] council". During construction of what was to become Willoughby Hall, the architects, now known as Williamson, Faulkner Brown and Partners, were commissioned to design two further halls, Cavendish [77] and Ancaster. All demonstrate a Scandinavian provenance, particularly in

Fig. 77
*Cavendish Hall
Architect: Williamson
Faulkner Brown and Partners
1966*

their simple organisation and low-pitched copper roofs with projecting eaves, fashionable pursuits at the time of the competition, but somewhat outworn *motifs* when completed in 1966.

Other notable forays into modernism during the 1960s included a new building for social sciences by Bartlett and Gray, completed in 1967, and Cripps Health Centre by Cartwright, Woollatt and Partners, completed a year later and to which the £100,000 donation for a university chapel had been diverted. The Social Sciences building is a not undistinguished design within a courtyard typology, with three-storey flat-roofed blocks in brick and exposed concrete floor slabs. A central foyer with a complex system of stairs and ramps to

accommodate a sloping site gives access to heavily-textured concrete lecture theatres expressed externally as a separate entity. These are a fitting, if slightly modish response to the location.

The Cripps Health Centre enjoys a commanding position downhill from Cripps Hall **[78]**. Although relatively small in size, the architects have imparted to the building an appropriately enhanced scale by expressing the ponderous rhythm of a robust concrete frame which at the upper level defines a series of open terraces for undergraduates' convalescence and at the same time frames views to the south towards the river Trent. The critic, Reyner Banham, famously referred to this then fashionable device as "built-in bomb damage".

But much of the 1960s was dominated by establishing a medical school within the university, an aspiration first articulated as early as 1949. By mid-1964 the Minister of Health gave permission to proceed after support from Sheffield Regional Health Board had been established. In October of that year an advisory committee was set up within the university under Sir George Pickering to look at progressive medical education. The outcome was a radical proposal to integrate clinical and pre-clinical studies. Building Design Partnership of Preston, an *avant-garde* architectural firm which pioneered in Britain the cross-disciplinary practice of integrating the building professions within one organisation, were appointed to design the new teaching hospital and medical school on a site adjacent to and east of the existing campus. Designs were submitted in 1966. Massive resistance to the project from local residents resulted in a public enquiry which ultimately found in favour of the scheme. Construction began in 1969 and the Medical School was completed for the 1970/1971 session. However, one third of the cost was borne by the University thereby consuming much of its quinquennial budget.

As the 1970s loomed, no longer could architectural critics upbraid the universities for their singular conservatism in building procurement. As in most universities, modern architecture at Nottingham had come to stay and the view of The Architects' Journal that "a large number [of universities] have not learnt enough about architecture and planning" and "do not necessarily appreciate the full meaning of modern architecture . . . many appear to think of it merely as a style which is more fashionable than the traditional styles", no longer obtained.

But within half a decade the very tenets of modernism seemed under threat from a series of reactions to it. Like modernism, these reactionary movements which embraced so-called post-modernism, and vernacular and historical revivalism, were applied by a new generation of architects indiscriminately to any building type. But whereas modernism, particularly in its 'heroic' period between the wars, had been a crusading architectural mission transcending any notion of 'style', post-modernism, in its imported transatlantic guise, reduced architecture to a diverse mix of applied motifs, a freestyle culled from the entire pantheon of architectural history. Universities (including Nottingham) were not to escape from this thankfully short-lived architectural phenomenon, of which the Djanogly Arts Centre and Music Recital Hall, by the Graham Brown Partnership, are the most obvious manifestation.

Science and Engineering Buildings

Coincidentally with the publication of Jellicoe's campus plan of 1955, Basil Spence was appointed to prepare plans for a group of Faculty of Applied Science Buildings on the Clifton Boulevard site which had been acquired from the City in 1949. The site was occupied by a series of single-storey blocks leased back to the Ministry after purchase and it was the layout of these blocks which was to determine the siting of proposed engineering laboratories in Spence's plan so that phased demolition could be accommodated within the building programme. The first building to be completed was the Mining and Fluid Mechanics laboratory in 1960, by which time a fully developed plan for the site including photographs of a highly detailed model had been published in the January edition of the Architectural Review for that year.

Fig. 79
Coates Building
Architect: Basil Spence
(completed by Renton Howard
Wood Associates)
1965

Spence's initial proposals had been presented to the University in 1957 and the built outcome is very much as the developed scheme published in the *Architectural Review* over two years later. The plan is notable for its boldness; the attenuated three-storey Coates Building forms a barrier between the potentially noisy proposed engineering laboratory spurs to the south and the quiet pedestrianised soft landscaped courts to the north, and at the same time forms a symbolic 'wall' between the applied and pure science departments. The symbolic divide is further enhanced by an informal axis set up between the Science Library to the west and the tower to the east which effectively define the central space. Indeed, it is the careful relationship between buildings and open spaces which characterises Spence's plan and to which individual buildings remain subservient. Nowhere else at Highfields was such a satisfactory urban outcome to be achieved although such an aspiration had been central to the plans of Thomas (1949), Jellicoe (1955) and McMorran (1958).

In essence, Spence was reiterating well-tried techniques: a series of flat-roofed rectilinear blocks of three to four storeys arranged in a loosely orthogonal manner, but without any strong axial relationships, to enclose a series of linked open spaces. Moreover, some of the buildings enclosed their own private courtyards so that a clear hierarchy of open space from public to private domains was established.

Although conforming to the overall plan, the individual buildings, whilst adhering to a five-foot modular grid, are sufficiently diverse in their architectural expression and in their use of materials to avoid any hint of excessive repetition. This variety was to some extent an inevitable outcome of Spence's policy of giving young architects a free hand in designing individual buildings within the constraints of the overall plan, but at another level reflects Spence's eclectic tendencies, his predilection for the picturesque, and his deep understanding of traditional building materials and their detailing.

Pope Building
Coates Building

Although now named after distinguished professors of engineering, the Pope and Coates Buildings, designed by Basil Spence, were for many years designated simply T1 (Teaching One) and T2 respectively. Together they form a dramatic building group where diverse modernist principles are clearly articulated. The Coates Building, completed in 1965 by Renton, Howard, Wood Associates, presents an attenuated three-storey north elevation to a central landscaped court [79] and a corresponding four-storey elevation to the noisy service areas and workshop spurs to the south [80]. The elevations are dominated by uninterrupted 'strip' windows linked by Derbyshire stone spandrel cladding panels looking for all the world like an apotheosis of Le Corbusier's Villa Stein of 1927. The recessed ground floor behind free-standing reinforced concrete columns or *pilotis* merely serves to reinforce the Corbusian reference. Entrances to departments within this linear block are marked by voids at ground floor level with associated cantilevered canopies which seem to 'hover' without any obvious visible means of support. Moreover, the whole building appears to float on a huge ground beam, suggesting other modernist pursuits: the disassociation, visually, of building and site, and the clear expression of subsidiary elements like entrances, canopies and staircases.

Fig. 80
Coates Building
Architect: Basil Spence
(completed by Renton Howard
Wood Associates)
1965

Another concern of modernists was the correspondence between internal and external spaces and Spence achieves this with spectacular success in the interface between the Coates and Pope Buildings; a three-storey high exhibition space occupies a trapezoidal plot between its two neighbours to form an exhibition gallery, the architectural *tour de force* of the whole science complex [81]. Vast expanses of glazed curtain walling not only afford generous levels of daylighting, but ensure a powerful relationship with adjacent soft landscaping and formal pools. Internally the spatial drama is heightened by galleries overlooking the central space and by a freestanding central staircase, like a huge piece of abstract sculpture, suspended from the roof structure by slender steel sections. In its generous use of hardwoods and in the delicacy of its detailing, this exhibition space evokes yet another tradition in modern architecture, that of Scandinavia, which, in its concern for natural materials, articulated a new architecture well removed from the machine aesthetic promoted on the Continent. The latter tradition was applied equally successfully by Spence to the spurs of engineering laboratories, evoking Mies van der Rohe's buildings for the Illinois Institute of Technology (1939-1956) in Chicago.

To the north of the exhibition hall, the Pope Building, completed in 1961, offers yet another building typology, the courtyard plan. Cellular spaces are arranged around a small carefully landscaped courtyard, emerging as a concealed oasis within the complex. Spence also rings the changes in elevational treatment: glazed curtain walling originally revealed the raked floors of back-to-back lecture theatres on both elevations.

Chemistry Building
Physics and
Mathematics Building

Like the Pope Building, Spence's Chemistry Building, completed in 1961, adopts the courtyard plan, accentuating the fact by associating the courtyard and entrance. Elevations clearly express a three-storey concrete framed structural bay with infill of glazing and brickwork. The brickwork panels are separated from the structural columns by vertical slots of glazing, thereby emphasising the brickwork's non-structural role as a cladding device.

To the northeast, the Physics and Mathematics Building of 1963, completed by Renton, Howard, Wood Associates, presents yet another planning typology; two three-storey linear blocks set at right angles to form an entrance foyer at their junction. This space is an 'interface' acting between the two blocks with exactly the same architectural intent as the exhibition space between the Coates and Pope Buildings, where equally, spatial drama had been extracted from the deployment of staircases, landings and associated galleries. Moreover the transparency of the original glazed curtain wall (now sadly removed) contrasted with the solidity of elevational treatment to the rest of the building; full height brickwork panels which deny any structural expression alternate with vertical strips of glazing and spandrel panels between.

Science Library
Tower Building

Although Andrew Renton, as Spence's associate, had been closely involved with the science buildings since inception in 1957, he left Spence's office long before the complex of buildings was complete to set up in practice in his own right as

Renton, Howard, Wood Associates. In this guise he was to complete commissions originally procured by Spence, so it is hardly surprising that in retrospect, given Renton's provenance, the change of hand appears imperceptible. But late commissions, particularly the tower building and science library, both completed in 1964, exhibit a move away from the smooth aesthetic of Spence's earlier work to a more robust architectural expression, more in tune with the contemporaneous products of the so-called English Brutalists. Like the Brutalists, and indeed, the American architect Paul Rudolph, Renton was to explore a heavily textured and modelled architecture first in the Science Library and tower building, and subsequently, if less successfully, in the Psychology Building.

The Science Library occupies a commanding site overlooking the principal open space which terminates at the tower building opposite **[82]**. It is an in-situ three storey concrete-framed structure where columns at close centres are expressed as projecting 'fins' with a granite aggregate finish, as are the spandrel panels between. Access to a compact and well organised plan is gained via a three-storey high, top-lit void, the most dramatic architectural intervention in an otherwise rather bland affair.

But the pursuit of a more robust architectural expression is much more successful at the tower building. Although the tower had always been a dominant component of the 1957 Spence plan **[83]**, Renton changed the orientation to north-south (with, incidentally, disastrous solar heating

Fig. 83

*Tower Building
with Chemistry Building
Perspective drawing by
Basil Spence
1957*

*Architect: Basil Spence
succeeded by
Renton Howard Wood
Associates
1957-69*

consequences for the accommodation of southerly aspect) and associated the tower with a podium, reflecting a 'tower-and-podium' orthodoxy established at Lever House, New York, by Gordon Bunshaft of Skidmore, Owings and Merrill in 1952.

Where the American prototype had been monumental, however, Renton's version at Nottingham is of surprisingly delicate scale imparted largely by the small structural bay expressed throughout its sixteen storeys. The plan is a typical 'racetrack' affair and highlights the building's major flaw. Because the building has a relatively small 'footprint' which needs to accommodate centrally-positioned lavatories, lifts and stairs (which cannot be miniaturised), the remaining depth of usable floorspace is minimal, leading to a lack of flexibility. But externally, the tower subtly manipulates solid and void into a highly sophisticated architectural composition. The building sits in a depression, concealing the column bases, so that the tower appears to 'hover', emerging weightlessly from the site. The first two floors are recessed behind free-standing *pilotis* **[84]** and thereafter each successive group of three storeys is expressed flush to or recessed from the structure, imparting a characteristic deeply profiled modelling to the elevations which come alive in oblique sunlight **[85]**. The blank end elevations are divided by a deeply recessed glazed slot to the escape stairs. By way of contrast to the highly textured tower, the top-lit podium workshop is clad in smooth Staffordshire blue brickwork.

Psychology Geology and Cell Biology Building Pharmacy Building

Like the Coates Building, the Psychology, Geology, and Cell Biology Building (as designated when built) of 1967 by Renton, Howard, Wood Associates,

Fig. 84
*Tower Building
Architect: Renton Howard
Wood Associates
1964*

Fig. 85
*Tower Building
Architect: Renton Howard
Wood Associates
1964*

accommodates a series of teaching departments within a massive linear block which also forms a physical barrier between the engineering workshops and the public park to the west. The block runs into the contours but maintains a constant eaves height to give four storeys at its southern end and three to the north. The entrance to Psychology at first floor level from a massively scaled stair sits under a cantilevered lecture theatre forming a canopy clad in precast granite aggregate concrete panels **[86]**, reflected in another similarly clad lecture theatre further up the slope at ground floor level. The interface between this and the linear block forms an entrance

to Pharmaceutical Science. Externally, the linear block of cellular accommodation is robustly expressed in brick bays which effectively conceal any structure, only a hint of structural columns being given by a recessed vertical rendered strip between projecting brick piers at every bay. The effect is singularly ponderous and contrasts sharply with the litheness of the Coates Building alongside.

Hallward Library

Since the Jellicoe plan of 1955 (in which the Trent Building was to be reordered as a library), the whole question of a new library for the University, what form it

Fig. 86

Psychology Geology and Cell Biology Building Entrance to Psychology Architect: Renton Howard Wood Associates 1967

should take and where it should be sited, remained constantly on senate's agenda. By the time of their appointment as architects for the new building in 1963, Williamson, Faulkner Brown and Partners had not only gained a national reputation for progressive library buildings, but were also engaged in developing their winning entries for the competition staged in 1950 to design a group of halls of residence, ultimately to be known as Willoughby, Cavendish and Ancaster.

After abandoning the library scheme for the Trent Building, a site to the north of the Portland Building was proposed before settling for its present location. In retrospect, it seems fitting that arguably

the best example of progressive architecture at Highfields should not only provide a potent symbol for the University's well-established academic ambition, but should also occupy the most prominent site on campus in terms of its central location and its commanding elevation.

When completed for the 1973 session by the re-fashioned practice of Faulkner-Brown, Hendy, Watkinson and Stonor, the Hallward Library for arts and social sciences represented the 'state of the art' for academic libraries in Britain [87]. During the decade between appointment and completion on site, the architect Faulkner-Brown and the then-librarian, Dick Smith, had, during their researches visited the most up-to-date academic libraries in the United States, and much of the strategic planning of the Hallward building reflects contemporaneous transatlantic practice. The most obvious manifestations of this are flexible open planning where areas of differing functions are delineated by free-standing furniture rather than by fixed partitions, and the decision to employ full air conditioning and permanent artificial lighting to serve a deep-plan configuration.

Within the open plan ethos, a largely open stack system is utilised with carefully defined 'closed' stack areas for archival and special collection material. The organisation of plan and section is a model of clarity: the building is effectively four storeys high, but a substantial cross-fall on site is utilised to provide the main access to the 'first' floor at grade. This means that the upper three floors can maintain the open plan by relegating closed stacks, the majority of cellular accommodation, service access and services to what is effectively a basement. The floor slab of the entrance

Fig. 87

Hallward Library
Architect: Faulkner-Brown,
Hendy, Watkinson and Stonor
1973

floor projects beyond the totally glazed curtain wall at this level, which, combined with judiciously placed earth mounds, allows the huge pavilion form of the library to appear to float above the site.

All major elements like catalogue, issue desk, exit control and central staircase are visible on entry to the open-plan ground floor. The two upper floors **[88]**,

also a model of rational planning, are open-planned with perimeter closed carrels to the east and west and open carrels to the north and south. Two 'cores' containing stairs and services impede minimally into the space.

A powerful unifying element of the interior spaces is the zigzag ceiling design which incorporates the permanent artificial lighting. The resultant coffers effectively raise the perceived ceiling height so that the typical oppressiveness of deep plan buildings is alleviated; moreover, glare is avoided because in normal use naked lighting sources are invisible. The unrelenting rigour of the building's organisation is relieved by lavish use of hardwood veneers internally for carrels, partitions and doors to give a balance of richness and texture. Similarly, the open carrels set at seventy degrees to the perimeter walls offer relief from the otherwise relentless orthogonal geometry.

Externally, the building clearly expresses its function and its organisation, a pursuit which was to inform many seminal works of modernism. By day or night the general activity of the entrance floor can be seen from outside. Similarly, students can be seen at work in the carrels, expressed by double height slit windows which occupy the interfaces between 'Cornish grey' pre-cast concrete cladding panels.

Although utterly different in its architectural provenance, the library may be perceived as extending a 'pavilion in the park' typology which informed the Highfields campus from the outset. Ironically, the library continues this typology more rigorously than did the prototypical Trent and Portland buildings, the latter, according to The Architects' Journal of January 9 1958, being "lavishly dug into the hillside."

When complete, the library was acclaimed by the architectural profession and critics alike. In 1974 the Royal Institute of British Architects' assessors were impressed by "a deep plan never oppressive . . . a warm and welcoming place that makes one want to work", when presenting their prestigious building award. And in the same year the Cement and Concrete Association's assessors trumpeted, "[the library is] a

strong and respectable neighbour to the many fashions of architecture to be found around it." But the last word surely went to transatlantic librarian, Keyes Metcalf, writing in The Architects' Journal of 24 April 1974. Clearly impressed by the building's North American provenance, he declared the library to be "a landmark in the history of academic library architecture in Great Britain."

Medical School

It was during Bertrand Hallward's Vice-Chancellorship, on 27 July 1964, that an announcement in the House of Commons signalled the foundation at Nottingham of the first new British medical school since the turn of the century. Its establishment, after many years of assiduous lobbying on Hallward's part, was to coincide with the design of a new 1200-bed district general hospital on a site adjacent to Highfields campus but separated from it to the east by a ring road. Both buildings were designed by Building Design Partnership. It had always been Hallward's intention that such a location, contiguous with other university facilities, would allow medical students to avail themselves fully of the intellectual, social and sporting life of the University.

After a protracted design period, including a public enquiry, the first pile for the Medical School was driven into the Clifton Boulevard site in May 1971. The Medical School was designed from the outset as an integral component of the new hospital structure which itself reflected progressive North American practice. The design strategy, which had been established in the mid-1960s, followed closely that of Britain's most ambitious hospital design to date at Greenwich by Howard Goodman.

Fig. 89
*Medical School
Architect: Building Design
Partnership
1975*

Goodman was the first British hospital architect to embrace the 'interstitial floor' concept which had been developed for hospital buildings in Canada and the United States. As its name suggests, the interstitial floor was an intermediate floor purely for services between usable flexible floorspace for the myriad of activities within a major teaching hospital. Such a device was seen as central to meeting the demands for flexibility in a modern hospital building by allowing for the modification or renewal of sophisticated mechanical and electrical plant without major disruption of a working building. It also recognised that the services of such a complex building type as a hospital would be outworn or obsolete long before its structure or envelope.

A previous postwar orthodoxy in hospital design had promoted high-rise solutions which led to less than satisfactory vertical relationships between major departments. At Nottingham, Building Design Partnership followed an emerging American model of medium-rise blocks forming courts and allowing for more appropriate horizontal inter-departmental relationships to be established. The architects were to pursue simultaneously at the Leeds teaching hospital a similar strategy which was to emerge as a norm for hospital planning in the 1970s.

Central to the design of what was to become the Queen's Medical Centre was the notion of a flexible 'system' of structure and services which could not only accommodate at the outset a hugely varied and complex brief, but could also respond to changes in use as patterns of medical care developed. In the event, the Medical School was to fit into this pre-determined organisation of building elements, reflecting a then-fashionable theoretical stance of 'architectural indeterminacy' which was seen to consume the building professions at the time. At its most extreme, it was considered perfectly acceptable within this theoretical construct for the hospital's chapel to occupy standard bays within the structure, and, indeed, to be served by identical fenestration to adjacent wards and medical departments. It was left to stained glass commissioned from the artist, Brian Clark, and inserted within the standard window 'system', to imbue the chapel with any sense of ecclesiastical presence.

Externally, the whole building is simply expressed by a recessed ground floor with exposed concrete columns and an infill of glazing and vertical stack-bonded blue brickwork **[89]**. At upper floors, continuous strip windows and buff brick spandrels oversail the columns and the interstitial service floors are discreetly marked by minimal openings of glazed louvres.

The medical school is marked within the repetitive courtyard typology of Queen's Medical Centre by a grand double-height entrance hall with an imposing spiral stair which unfortunately obscures Gillian Wise's celebrated abstract mural construction in stainless steel **[90]**. This installation reflects yet another architectural concern of the time: that major public buildings incorporate commissioned art works as an integral component of the fabric. An unremarkable and rather lumpen enclosed footbridge linking the Highfields campus to the Medical School seems a less than celebratory response to Hallward's vision of integrating the two sites both physically and symbolically.

Fig. 90
Medical School Entrance Hall with Sculpture by Gillian Wise Architect: Building Design Partnership 1975

Chapter 6
Recent Buildings

The Contextual Challenge

The development, during the last decade or so, of the Highfield's campus, as well as the outlying sites, has been marked by the lack of any coherent architectural plan. Much of the discussion in the previous chapters has been not so much to do with the aesthetics or the stylistic allusions of the various buildings which make up the University, but with the clarity of their plan and their relationship one to another, with the importance of views and vistas, of axis through, and of the arrangements of spaces between, buildings. For architecture is not about the imposition of a building upon a site as if it were flat and unencumbered, but rather about the development of that design to relate, either by continuity or by contrast, to its context.

The series of campus plans and the continual stop-start building programme which characterised much of the first forty years of the University's tenure of the Highfield's site, had led to a defracted and piecemeal collection of buildings. Some of the developments, like Cripps Hall are, of course, very distinguished. Others, like the Matlock Block at Derby Hall are insensitively sited, and must be as uncomfortable for their users as they are for their context. Recent benefactions and fund raising have allowed a number of designated buildings to be built, and it is these, perhaps due to their individuality more than anything, which tend to be noticeable. Yet these new buildings appear almost invariably to have been designed to express popular post-modern pursuits rather than any real concern for context or a unique "sense of place". Thus the need on the part of the University to provide a coherent policy for the repair and stitching together of the campus fabric is all the more important.

Fig. 91
Magnetic Resonance Imaging Building Architect: John Viner Associates 1991

Fig. 92
*Institute of Engineering,
Surveying and
Space Geodesy Building
Architect: James McCartney
1996*

The Arts Centre, Department of Music and Recital Hall have taken a prime position on the site of the former Lido. The Magnetic Resonance Imaging Building and the Institute of Engineering, Surveying and Space Geodesy sit on open sites flanking Cut Through Lane between Science City and Cripps Hall. Over the down, the East Midland Conference Centre is set on rising ground above Beeston Lane, and only the Swimming Pool is tucked away, almost invisible from the campus circulatory. All these buildings are very much individual statements yet only one, the Swimming Pool, makes any real contribution to its context. It is the one building which, paradoxically, does not make reference in its style or materials to the buildings around it or to the perceived nature of the University's architecture, but nevertheless exhibits the most fitting response to its site.

As for the others, the MRI Building, by John Viner Associates, sits well enough atop its hill but ignores its delicate relationship with Cripps Hall, to which it turns its distended rear end [91]. In so doing it disassociates itself from its site and is forced to remind visitors of its entrance by peeling back the brickwork to reveal a whimsical steel structure beneath an ordinary, pitched roof. Lower down the hill, James McCartney's IESSG Building appears unrelated to anything around it, a flat-site building cut into the hillside and addressing, in a linear fashion, the road and the high ground beyond [92]. It is a long, spinal building treated almost strictly as elevation, with a tall recessed bay incorporating not the entrance, as might be expected, but a curious, rounded stair tower which is set deep and penetrates the roof as an observation room. The entrance is through what should be a

Fig. 93
*Wolfson Building Materials
Engineering and
Materials Design
Architect: Crampin Pring
McCartney
1998*

ground floor office window, if the rhythm of the exterior glazing along the main façade were acknowledged. An addition to the south, being built at the time of writing, doubles the depth of the building at its eastern end and converts that elevation from a rather mundane affair with a lean-to roof to something more dramatic, presenting a v-shaped roof and a valley gutter in profile. For all their short-comings, however, these two buildings make an architectural response. The East Midlands Conference Centre, designed by the Directorate of Works as the Jesse Boot Centre in 1984, and extended by Maber Associates in 1994, is only remarkable for its banality.

The argument, for a critic, should not be one of mere style but of appropriateness, judged in terms of architectural syntax and contextual response, of form and of function. And here the absence of any strong architectural leadership has led only to confusion, a lack of rigour and a touch of hubris.

It is, rather surprisingly, in the small and apparently insignificant additions and infills that some of the best recent architecture is to be found. The addition to Materials Engineering and Materials Design (The Wolfson Building) in Science City by Crampin, Pring, McCartney is a neat, wrap-around design in sheet steel

Fig. 94

Institute of Architecture Gallery Architect: Martin Noutch 1997

and crisply detailed, well-mannered brickwork **[93]**. It tidies up what was an ugly corner and provides an exciting indoor atrium space between the new teaching areas and the exterior wall of the old building. At Lenton Firs, now home to the School of the Built Environment, Martin Noutch's long, elegant and economic exhibition gallery makes a simple statement in well-detailed brick and timber, as well as bringing some life into the previously dead teaching

spaces which it adjoins **[94]**. This is just the first part of a phased scheme which, as the Marmont Centre for Renewable Energy, will eventually enclose three sides of the lawn to create an open quadrangle. At an even smaller scale, a canopy and a new entrance lobby at Sherwood Hall suddenly make sense of a circulation system which, through alterations over the years, had lost any clarity; small alterations perhaps, but they are handled with some care and to enormous effect.

Fig. 95
Djanogly Arts Centre and Music Recital Hall Architect: Graham Brown Partnership 1993

Fig. 96

Djanogly Arts Centre and
Music Recital Hall
Architect: Graham Brown
Partnership
1993

Djanogly Arts Centre and Music Recital Hall

The most significant addition to the Highfields campus since the completion of the Portland Building was the new Arts Centre and Music Recital Hall, a complex of buildings accommodating the Departments of Art History and Music, the University Art Gallery, the Visitors' Centre, a bookshop and a café. With the exception of the Trent and Portland Buildings, no other single building on the campus is so noticeable. It is the one building which provides the interface between the town and the gown, the one building which marks the main entrance to the campus [95], the one building which is accessible to the

public on demand and which, by its very nature as much as the facilities it provides, needs to impart an impression of the aspirations of the seat of learning which it represents. This is a very tall order and therefore the building must be considered very critically. So does the Arts Centre and Djanogly Recital Hall meet these demands?

In assuming the site of the Lido, it would appear that the architects, the Graham Brown Partnership, assumed also its scale and style. For the new complex is a series of low, connected pavilions in a post-modern Tuscan style. The complex comprises three main parts: the public spaces and Department of Art History arranged like a basilica with nave and side aisles; the Art History lecture theatre and slide library arranged as a rotunda; and the Department of Music and the Recital Hall, arranged around three sides of an open quadrangle like monastic buildings, a "dormitory" on two sides and a "great hall" on the third. The references are certainly cultured, as befits this oasis of the arts stranded between Science City and the Science Park. But the architecture demonstrates little understanding of its provenance.

This linear plan of a basilica demands the dominance of the nave **[96]**. But this is denied, for the art gallery, which colonises the central space, is divided into two rooms by a cross passage which goes nowhere: the doors giving onto it appear to be permanently locked. Had this been a transept, into which the space could flow, it would have made syntactical sense. But that is not the case. The side aisles, containing both the Visitors' Centre and Art History's offices and studios, are sometimes a large lean-to and sometimes a long passage with cells off. The result is an extraordinary imbalance between one aisle and the other, the intimate nature of the Art History Department compared with the openness of the Visitors' Centre, where the side wall is peeled away to reveal a glazed gallery. Externally, despite this revelation, the suggestion is of a large,

Fig. 98

Djanogly Arts Centre and
Music Recital Hall
Architect: Graham Brown
Partnership
1993

single volume, for the clerestory which runs from one gable end to the other suggests no subdivisions. Yet the nave, as has been noted, is two volumes and the narthex, containing the café, flanked by an entrance lobby and kitchen on one side, and the bookshop on the other, is as wide as the nave and half the side aisles as well. It is a tall, ungainly space with an inelegant, exposed steel structure and a sweeping panoramic bay window

overlooking a duckpond at the south end. If this were a baptismal niche, the water would be over-abundant.

The rotunda **[97]** is set on axis with the central line of the basilica, a relationship unknown in architectural history where Early Christian churches would adopt one or the other of these forms, but not both. Although not freestanding, for it is linked by low passageways north and south, it nevertheless reads as a discrete element, the circular form of the parapet wall and conical roof being clearly expressed. The rotunda form suggests an open space within, subdivided, if necessary, radially, and perhaps with rooms arranged centrifugally. But no, this space is split by a diameter which continues the central axis of the basilica, resulting in two D-shaped rooms. And as in the Visitors' Centre, the room on the west, the slide library, is revealed when the brick wall is peeled away to create a cloister which has no apparent function and is largely inaccessible.

In building the quadrangle **[98]**, the architects have had to accommodate the widely differing scales of offices and teaching rooms, and a recital hall. But rather than expressing each element individually, as might be done traditionally in monastic buildings, they have fused large volumes with small, layered roofs and adopted lean-tos. The result is a confusion of scales, from the low, protruding entrance porch to the massive dominance of the hall on one side. Internally, there is little clarity in the plan. The function of the hall is indicated by the blank walls and high-level roundels, but the exact size and positioning of this space within its enclosure is ambiguous. The entrance hall is another west-facing glazed gallery, a reception area perhaps but no introduction to the building, for it is a terminal space rather than the start of an architectural promenade. And above, what would appear, from the window arrangement, to be linear passageways turn out to be cellular offices.

It is axiomatic that if allusion is made to an historical architecture, then the language of that architecture needs to be understood. It does not need to be followed, for Mannerism thrived upon contradiction, but it did so knowingly. This building remains completely inarticulate. Externally, the Djanogly Art Centre and Music Recital Hall is neatly built and well finished. The Italianate references apparent in the plan are expressed elevationally in pedimented gables, polychromatic banding and a pantile roof. There is even a little bellcote above one gable end. Had Morley Horder's Lido not been a long, low, Tuscan building, would Graham Brown's replacement have been anything different? At least there might not have been the flag-waving, tubular steel entrance structure: a diving board without a pool.

The Djanogly Art Centre and Music Recital Hall is a real and metaphorical gateway to the University. Yet, being so long and low, it is wrongly scaled, and being so historically inaccurate is academically embarrassing. This is all perhaps because it is a building too caught up in its past. The history of its site, and of the lake and former Tea Pavilion opposite, is contentious and, until recently, has been one of constant discussion between the University, who wanted to own it, and the City, who did. In replacing the Lido, the University provided, perhaps at the direction of the city planners, more of the same: a suggestion of continuity with the past, perhaps for the benefit of the public, rather than a statement of the future intent of a seat of learning, which is what the Trent Building had first provided in 1928. In failing to respond, as a "marker" building, to the significance of the south entrance and to the scale of the Trent and Portland Buildings beyond, the Djanogly Art Centre and Music Recital Hall represents an opportunity missed. Perhaps the new D H Lawrence archive building, designed, as the result of an architectural competition, to replace the ill-fated Lakeside Pavilion, will do something to adjust this imbalance.

Fig. 99
Swimming Pool
Architect: Faulkner Browns
1996

Sports Hall and Swimming Pool Day Nursery

Morley Horder's Lido, although built on ground belonging to the City of Nottingham, had always provided the University with a facility much appreciated albeit for the summer months alone. But its closing in the late 1980s and eventual demolition to make room for the Djanogly Art Centre and Music Recital Hall left the campus with no place for students or staff to swim. The building of the Sports Centre at the north east corner of the campus in 1970, and the subsequent provision of an all-weather playing field, provided a focus for sporting activities and, following the demise of the Lido, the most obvious siting for a new swimming pool. But the Sports Hall was a building which did little for itself and nothing for its site. The main steel structure was purchased, second hand, at a cost of £177,000, from a site in Shropshire, in 1968, and rebuilt by F S Eales. Clad in brown brick, it is a barn of a building, the only articulation being the twenty two tall buttresses which subdivide its length and support the open steel trusses of the roof. It was subsequently extended in 1976 and 1983, but despite this, the building failed to provide any sense of place and succeeded only in appearing as a large,

lumpen mass emerging from the trees. As the location for the bi-annual degree ceremonies, it is unprepossessing.

The positioning of the new Swimming Pool, on axis across the car park from the main entrance to the Sports Hall, and the location of the new Day Nursery at the far end of the space, succeeds in tying in the Sports Hall with its site and providing a complex of buildings which offer, if not

Fig. 100
Swimming Pool
Architect: Faulkner Browns
1996

gravitas, at least a sense of place. This is because attention is now drawn away from the large, gable end of the Sports Hall with its vulgar, over-scaled lettering, and towards the long side elevation, previously inconsequential but now purposeful.

The Swimming Pool, designed by Faulkner Browns, was opened in 1996 [99]. It is not a large building, the pool itself being only 25m by 16m, but it is positioned on raised ground and treated with a sense of scale that gives it presence. The white steel and milky turquoise glass render it noticeable, and at night, set within the trees, it glows with an inner light. The approach to the building is up a long ramp, set in line with the covered entrance to the Sports Centre. This axis is carried right through the building, from the canopied double doors, through the small, tidy lobby, to the centre lane of the pool, with the translucent, poly-carbonate barrel vault above [100], to the scoreboard on the far wall. The exposed steel structure picks up the symmetry, a series of eight pin-jointed portal frames, the joints lining up beneath the barrel vault. The steel frame is clearly stated, the flanges deep and the bolt connections well-expressed. Externally, the frames are dramatised, for, from the shoulder of each one extends upwards a curving arm supporting steel louvres, a *brise soleil* against the low morning and evening sun [101]. From inside the pool, the frame reads clearly through the glazing, the milky turquoise panels pulling back to reveal each stanchion, and a strip of clear glass is retained near to floor level to allow swimmers a glimpse of the treetops beyond and the low morning or evening sun.

The symmetry and rhythm of the steel stucture is reflected on plan. On entering,

the first two bays are given over to administration rooms on the left and changing rooms on the right. The next four bays contain the pool, and the final bay, behind the score board, is the plant room. If there are inconsistencies in the remarkably well ordered arrangement of this building, it is here. For while the internal arrangement of the bays suggest a rhythm of 2-4-1, the external expression is of 2-3-2: open, cross-braced, and open again. Furthermore, the symmetrical arrangement of the plan might suggest, in the nature of balance, the symmetry of the sexes. Thus on entering the building, the response is to turn one way for the men's changing room, or to turn the other way for the women's. In the event, the changing room is mixed (although cubicles provide privacy) and all to one side. This is perhaps as much a reflection of the informality of modern life as it is the need for economical plumbing.

The third building in this complex, the Day Nursery, was opened in 1995. Designed by Franklin Ellis, it appears from the outside to be a bungaloid, pitched roofed box, the only clue to its use being the orange columns which mark the green, glazed entrance. Internally, colour abounds and the scale diminishes to that of the little people who use it. It is a tight building and for adults must, at times, be awkward. But the variety of shapes evident in the plan - polygonal hallways, square window bays, funny corners here and there - make it a place of small-scale incidents and accidents to which the toddlers can relate. Windows at skirting level and low porthole lights in the doors impart an appropriately intimate scale. But it must be a reflection of our times that this building offers so little to the passer by. High fences enclose the playground and the blank brickwork turns a cold face to the campus. All the joy is kept inside.

Fig. 101
Swimming Pool
Architect: Faulkner Browns
1996

Food Science Building
Sutton Bonington

Any sense of order in the site plan at Sutton Bonington was lost when the north/south cross-campus road was closed. The road had given purpose to the positioning of Basil Spence's North Laboratory building and had separated the teaching from the largely administrative and residential area defined by the Main Building, and Rempstone, Kingston and Normanton Houses. At the narrowest point where the road had passed between the two, the University's Works Department built the octagonal, diminutive dining hall, with its brick piers and modish, laminated timber portal frame. It not only bridged the gap and closed off the through-vista, but produced a confusion of geometries in an otherwise largely orthogonal site plan which was further confounded by the building of the elaborately echeloned James Cameron-Gifford library nearby. The result of all this careless infilling is depressing.

It would seem then, that the chance to start afresh in the open space to the east, would have been welcomed and acted upon by any architect. Indeed, the South Laboratory Building, with its three storeys of coffered, pre-cast concrete wall panels, provides a bright and refreshing addition of some visual clarity. And so, one would think, does the new Food Sciences Building, built by L J Multon in 1997.

The Food Sciences Building sits behind and to one side of Spence's long block, and is set parallel to the South Laboratory Building. It is a large pavilion set in an open landscape and is visible from all sides. Aware of its prominence, the architects have treated it with some style: an almost pedimental elevation and ten peripteral columns suggest an ancient arcadian temple, while the use of green steel and black glass indicate a temple to science. Its

symmetry speaks of order and so its central atrium comes as no surprise. The strength of the building is in the clarity of its *parti,* but having established that, the architects lose control.

The main problem with the Food Sciences Building is in the entrance promenade. Although positioned centrally, the main doors are crushed up against the protruding block of the lecture theatre which is set at first floor level, in one corner of the main façade, and arranged diagonally to the line of the plan. It is too important a space not to pick up on the line of the main axis and could have very well extended as a central canopy above the entrance. Inside, the entrance hall terminates in the elevator shaft. There is no indication of the atrium space beyond and this is only found on climbing the stairs which wrap around the back of the shaft. The elevator could have been to one side and an axial, through-vista retained. The atrium, surrounded by a gallery, is pleasant enough, and lit from above by a long, curved, polycarbonate, rooflight. The curve of the roof follows the line of five great, bowed steel trusses, which are supported on columns along each side of the atrium and extend beyond the building's envelope to rest on the circular, concrete towers which march down either side of the building like so many Doric columns [102]. But this is a conceit which seems redundant, for little weight can bear upon these towers. Although they serve to support spiral escape stairs, the towers are curious for each is a hollow shaft (providing space for vent stacks) and capped by a saucer-like dome. They contain gas canisters which presumably need to be located outside the building. Temple columns to some, a means of escape to others: but for many at Sutton Bonington they must read like a row of grain silos - a suitably agricultural metaphor.

Postscript

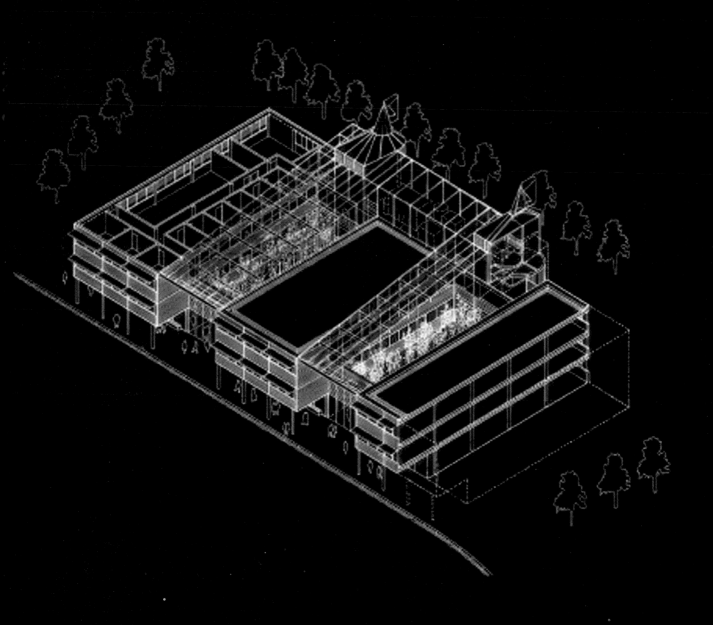

Historically, the most significant event since the granting of the University of Nottingham's Charter in 1948 has been the acquisition of land from a disused Raleigh Industries gearbox factory at Triumph Road to form a second campus. The potential for expansion that the six hectare new campus offers is central to Vice-Chancellor Sir Colin Campbell's vision for the next century and offers at this juncture in an established university's history, a fitting symmetry with Bertrand Hallward's vision for a new foundation in 1948. Whereas Hallward's ambition in a period of postwar austerity was to develop a university of national distinction in a context of rapid expansion in higher education, Campbell's ambitions lie in the global arena where key players in the increasingly competitive field of higher education are measured by international rather than national ranking.

When fully developed, the new campus will allow for a potential expansion of the University to twenty thousand students. Such ambition demanded a suitable architectural response and in pursuit of this, Sir Colin Campbell instituted a major international architectural competition for the Triumph Road site in 1996. Unusually for such events, the University invested significantly in formulating a detailed brief and in suitable honoraria for the six shortlisted competitors, five of whom submitted fully developed proposals. Given the pluralist state of late-twentieth century British architecture, the entries were appropriately diverse in the nature and ambition of their architectural solutions.

Two entrants, Fielden Clegg Design, and MacCormac, Jamieson and Pritchard based their schemes on a linear building typology, with an enclosed 'street'

providing access to all accommodation and running the entire length of the site, in the mistaken belief that all university activity can be programmed into such an attenuated building form. By contrast, the winning entry by Michael Hopkins and Partners, makes overt references to the existing campus by effecting a close correspondence between landscape and buildings [103]. It represents a bold planning strategy for a linear urban site which occupies a critical interface between the 'soft edge' of suburbia and Nottingham's inner city. Moreover, the site offers severe and apparently conflicting constraints: to the north-east the massive presence of monumental bonded warehousing and to the west the domestic scale of manicured suburban gardens.

But the most striking feature of Hopkins' plan and central to its organisation is a linear lake which forms a 'buffer' between the suburban 'edge' and the new university buildings. Furthermore, evoking a powerful memory of the Highfields campus, the architects have achieved a profound relationship between landscape and architecture not only by the judicious siting of individual buildings within the man-made landscape, but also by the simple device of a lakeside promenade which dramatically engages major pedestrian movement with key elements of building, planting and water.

Inevitably, within the competition system, as a more detailed brief emerges from dialogue between successful competitor and client, so the architectural solution is refined and modified; the potent architectural gesture of the drum-like library sited within the lake has been replaced by an inverted cone with spiral ramp circulation to segmental reading spaces, study carrels and

bookstacks, but still axially related to a public square and lecture theatres **[104]**. Flanking on both sides are the lakeside teaching departments; student housing for undergraduates and postgraduates now clad in brick, is situated towards the site periphery. The principal entrance to the site employs formal avenues as a 'prelude' to the campus proper, evoking another familiar memory, that of the Nottingham 'boulevard'.

Developing a strategy for energy-efficient 'green' buildings established at his celebrated Nottingham Inland Revenue headquarters, Hopkins has convincingly utilised 'thermal chimney' devices in the teaching buildings as a significant component of their architectural expression. Modernists had always decreed that overt display of a building's function and structure should constitute a primary generator of formal expression, but the teaching blocks at the new campus extend this condition onto a truly innovative 'green' architecture, to which the architects have applied the epithet 'eco-functionalism'.

Whilst the whole gamut of familiar 'green' devices such as louvres, light shelves, and internally exposed thermal mass (concrete structure) has been deployed, the real innovation has been to harness solar energy via photovoltaic cells incorporated within the atrium roofs for mechanically-powered heating and cooling in the extremes of winter and summer. Meanwhile, the rotating thermal chimneys turn according to wind direction and create negative pressure to assist air extraction **[105]**. Moreover, the southern elevations to the teaching blocks which address the lake,

Fig. 104

*New Campus
developed scheme
Architect: Michael Hopkins
and Partners
1998*

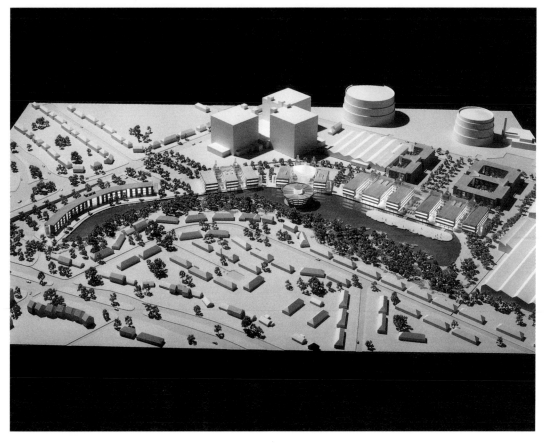

Fig. 105
*New Campus Teaching Building
axonometric drawing
by James Baker
Architect: Michael Hopkins
and Partners
1998*

incorporate 'scoops' at eaves level, expressed as giant cornices, so that prevailing winds cooled by passing over the adjacent lake, can enter the atria further to enhance summer cooling [106]. The roof surfaces also incorporate maintenance-free planting including a range of dwarf grasses, offering a habitat to supplement a 'wildlife belt' of mature trees at the western boundary.

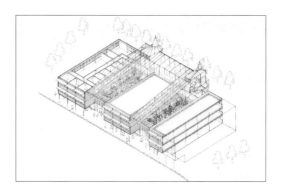

Taking clues from his recent *oeuvre* of overtly crafted buildings, Hopkins has employed a limited palette of traditional materials, notably brick and cedar cladding, as a further reminder of High-fields precedent. But by juxtaposing such traditional cladding with galvanised steel and concrete, Hopkins extends a quintessentially English notion of modernism, whilst offering at the same time a telling comparison with Spence's equally progressive (for his day) buildings at Science City.

Beyond the prosecution of the new campus plan there remains the perennial question of how the obvious environmental benefits afforded by a mature Highfields campus can be maintained and enhanced. Essentially, the new campus will prevent overcrowding by releasing approximately 8,000 square metres of accommodation on the existing campus. In turn this will allow for the long overdue demolition of temporary single-storey buildings at the Clifton Boulevard site and Cherry Tree Buildings behind the Portland Building, the latter allowing, finally, the potential for developing a recognisable urban space, or 'University Square', thereby realising the central recommendation of every university master planner since Sir Percy Thomas in 1949.

The creation of such an urban focus of civic dimensions in what was essentially an arcadian idyll had variously exercised the minds of campus planners at High-fields. Thomas had proposed an entirely inappropriate open space of huge size (which ignored the natural topography of the site) surrounded by buildings of equally heroic scale; in 1955 Jellicoe had profoundly modified Thomas' scheme, replacing the vast formal open space with a more fitting botanical garden laid out geometrically; even McMorran's more modest, but profoundly contextual design of 1958 failed to materialise. But such a cleared site to the rear of the Portland Building could dramatically re-establish the potential for realising a sheltered open space as a focus for social intercourse amongst the academic community.

Given that the new campus establishes a 'lung' for university expansion, it is unlikely that any major new building work, save for the creation of the new central area, will take place at Highfields. Such a course would inevitably result in over-development with a consequent erosion of environmental quality. The whole ambience of a mature landscape harbouring an architecturally diverse mix of buildings has been central to the University's development since inception and it is hardly surprising that the conservation, repair and renewal of buildings and landscape at Highfields collectively represent a major priority for the future. All of these pursuits involve

Fig. 106
w Campus Teaching Building
ectional perspective drawing
by James Baker
rchitect: Michael Hopkins and
Partners
1998

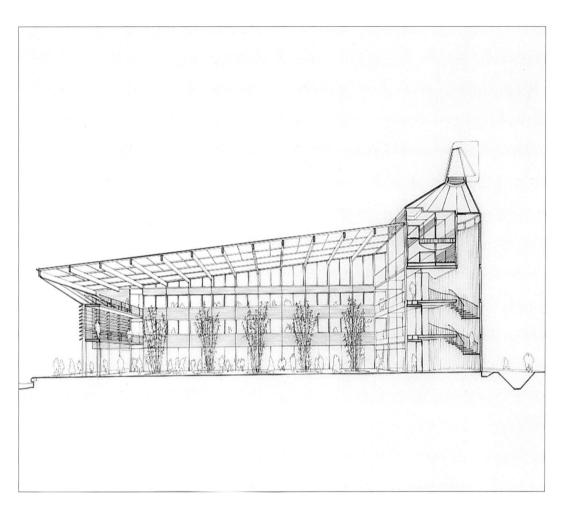

not only a sensitivity to what exists but also highly developed design skills to renew and reorder an existing building stock. This is particularly so for buildings by, for example, McMorran, Spence, or Renton, which are archetypical of their respective *genres.*

So, given half a century of campus architecture at the University of Nottingham, what sort of judgement emerges? Certainly, as the references to contemporaneous architectural journals reveal, the pundits were consistently less than enthusiastic about the University's cautious attitudes towards building procurement. But the world of architectural criticism, particularly in its immediately postwar guise, embraced a

notoriously monotheistic culture where buildings whose provenance was other than modernist, were doomed. By the 1970s, however, a fashionable concept of pluralism was to enter the architectural debate so that architectural critics were at last freed from the narrow creed of modernism. They enjoyed their new-found freedom and just as architects broadened their sources of architectural inspiration in a post-modern world, so did journalists re-discover a half-forgotten English eclectic tradition.

Consequently, the work of McMorran, O'Rorke and Howitt has undergone a long-overdue reappraisal which has not only restored the reputations of such architects, but has placed their buildings in a much wider art-historical perspective than any critic of the time would allow. This corpus of architecture at Highfields has emerged not only unscathed, but considerably enhanced from such renewed scrutiny – McMorran's work has gained Listed Building status – and now rightfully bears comparison with the more progressive contemporaneous output on campus from Basil Spence. Such a rehabilitation not only exposes the potential pitfalls of architectural dogma and the caprice of architectural criticism, but in the event is a telling reflection of the real nature of fifty years of architectural procurement at the University of Nottingham.

LIST OF PLATES

LIST OF FIGURES

Index